SUCCESS FREAK

KICK ASS IN LIFE [IN] 7 DAYS

BRUNO GRALPOIS

SUCCESS FREAK

FREAK

KICK ASS IN LIFE IN 7 DAYS

BRUNO GRALPOIS

BEAUFORT
BOOKS

For inquiries about volume orders, please contact:
Beaufort Books
27 West 20th Street, Suite 1102
New York, NY 10011
sales@beaufortbooks.com

Published in the United States by Beaufort Books
www.beaufortbooks.com

Distributed by Midpoint Trade Books,
a division of Independent Publishers Group
www.midpointtrade.com
www.ipgbook.com

Paperback ISBN: 9780825309281
Ebook ISBN: 9780825308123

Library of Congress Cataloging-in-Publication Data

Manufactured in the United States of America

To Success Freaks everywhere in the world.

And yes, that means you, too.

CONTENTS

ACKNOWLEDGMENTS

Every book is a journey worth taking along with friends and family. The source of my knowledge and inspiration comes from many anecdotal stories, professional experiences, and inspiring conversations with thought leaders, serial entrepreneurs, current and past colleagues, close friends, acquaintances—talented individuals who shared many success stories, and failures. All of them share a common passion for pursuing a more purposeful life.

I would like to express much gratitude to Christine Serb, for her support and encouragement. This book would not have been possible without inspiration and the care of friends, family, colleagues and avid supporters: Max and Anais Gralpois, Yves and Josette Gralpois, Danielle Touyre and Michelle Retif, Jerome

Retif, Alexandre Touyre, Laura Retif, Pierre Touyre, Stephanie Retif, and many great friends around the world - Florent Maillet, Jean-Charles Alvarez, Yannick Vadrot, Vivianne Arnold, Patricia Berns, Olivier Fontana, Matthew Cadman, and many others. They all contributed to making this book possible, providing feedback or encouragements. I also want to acknowledge the team at Hunt Marketing Group, especially Matt Hung, Heather Green, and Graham Herman for their efforts, and Josh Ellis, the Editor-in-Chief of *SUCCESS* Magazine, for his inspiring Foreword. I want to acknowledge a few other individuals: Daniel Fox, Martha Stewart, Bill Fritsch, Adam Mendoza, Keegan Hall, Alexis Williamson, the amazing team at Beaufort Books—Eric M. Kampmann, Megan Trank, Karen Hughes—as well as Laura Temple, Nia Martin, Allison Acton, and my loyal book agent, Bill Gladstone. They all share my vision for how *Success Freak* can help individuals in search of answers, inspiration, and guidance. They are hardcore Success Freaks.

FOREWORD

As Editor-in-Chief of *SUCCESS Magazine*, I received thousands of manuscripts from well intentioned, successful people who believed they had the insight and credibility to write the next great personal growth book. Most of them were derivative or based on some foolproof formula for earning riches and I never got past the first chapter of most of these books. But then again, I had never come across one in such a time of need. Maybe that's how you feel right now, too.

Luckily for both of us, *Success Freak* is different. This book is special, and Bruno is a unique voice in a crowded genre. An immigrant who came to America speaking barely any English, he leveraged the beliefs, habits, and skills set forth in this book to become one of the most impressive executives and business relationship gurus of our time, working with many of the world's most impactful companies—Microsoft, Visa, Verizon, and many others.

But this isn't some self-congratulatory autobiography. Bruno hardly mentions his own story in the book; it's not about him. It's about you and me.

To get us moving, he has put together a complete guide to success. This book contains actionable steps to go from a place of emptiness and unfulfillment to lives we love.

So often, personal growth books rely on time-worn tactics and self-evident truths that, while reliable, do nothing to provide the actual impetus to get us moving. Bruno goes beyond those, because—as he so clearly establishes—success is truly and deeply personal. It requires serious self-reflection and the willingness to change (and keep changing over the long haul).

The book is filled with insightful, inspiring quotes from some of the most impactful thinkers and doers of all time; each of these messages conveys exactly what we need to hear to get out of our own heads and realize that the challenges we face are so inherent to the human condition. These challenges are so often the impetus for great achievement.

Success Freak is special, because it has been constructed as a guide that focuses on the reader's personal evolution. Each chapter is accompanied by life-defining questions to ask yourself, and concrete, actionable steps that will transform your answers into the positive changes you seek. The order of operations Bruno lays out is crucial. This book will take you from defining what success means to you, to learning how to think and act differently; shift your mindset to overcome obstacles; push for results; capitalize on each day; fuel motivation from within; and recognize the opportunities around you. Mastery of the sometimes-unconventional habits laid out here (and explained in historical context) cannot fail you. They haven't failed me.

As I worked through the book, taking in a chapter a day, as Bruno suggests, I began to turn my mood and outlook around. Did I answer all my questions by Day Three? No, but I'd get started, gaining more clarity. Did I change my world by Day Five? No, but I'd gathered the energy to lay the foundation and get under way. Did I reach all my goals by Day Seven? No, but I was on the path to rebuilding my life to better than it was before, even more fulfilling and rewarding. I had a plan, and I've been acting on it. Where once I was worried about the future, now I'm thrilled to see what comes.

You'll feel the same way.

Very early in my tenure at the magazine, I established four tentpoles of *SUCCESS*, concepts all our readers could strive for that would create constant progress in their lives: Happiness; Health; Growth; Purpose. There are no limits to these concepts. If you're already happy, you can still become happier; health does not plateau; growth can be constant; and there is always a deeper meaning to be found. *Success Freak* will push you farther in the journey to those always-moving benchmarks than you ever thought possible. And when you reach the end, you'll look back and realize that the story has only begun.

It's your story. You're the main character. And it's up to you to decide the full arc of the narrative and how it ends.

But before any of that, no matter what you're going through in life, no matter where you've been, you must be ready to find out what comes next. Turn the page.

—JOSH ELLIS

EDITOR-IN-CHIEF *SUCCESS MAGAZINE*

UNLOCKING THE HIDDEN CODE OF SUCCESS

Since the dawn of time, leaders, scholars, scientists, and philosophers alike have sought to fully comprehend humankind's phenomenal adaptability and evolutionary success: the unrelenting human drive behind world conquests; the explorations of unknown lands and achievements few imagined possible.

Yet the feats of accomplished individuals in politics, sports, art, science, business, and other fields throughout history show empirical evidence of a burning desire to turn unfulfilled hopes into reality. The results of the ones who pursued a purposeful life—the ones who followed their dreams and worked tire-lessly—make up the world we know and enjoy today.

Their personal success stories fill our imagination and inspire us. Yet you may wonder: How did they do it? Why is success such an obsession in the first place? Let's be honest. We all want something more out of life. You wouldn't be reading this book otherwise. We all want to be extremely successful at what we do. "Good" is no longer good enough. Perhaps you hope to:

- Sky rocket your career or create a compelling future for yourself

- Start your own business and achieve financial freedom

- Feel happier or simply more fulfilled by pursuing your passion

- Influence others and make a lasting difference in their lives

- Light up that irresistibly vibrant spark inside of you

We want to be successful because of that inner drive, some-thing that we all feel in our gut, a sort of calling or craving that propels us forward. Our culture has always celebrated excep-tional people whose performance and life accomplishments are vastly superior to those of the rest of the population. We admire those who seem to be wildly successful to the naked eye. We envy them. We look up to them. We even idolize them and wonder, "What do they know that we don't? Are they geneti-cally predisposed to success, or is it the result of intense practice and extraordinary efforts?"

We define success narrowly as power, fame, or fortune. We tend to glorify those who have built massive financial empires, enjoy luxurious lifestyles, or are at the center of the media frenzy. We consider those individuals to be exemplary success stories. Their experience boils down to a single undeniable assertion: "Success" is indispensable social currency in modern times, and no one wants to be left out.

THE NEW CURRENCY OF OUR TIMES

However, as is true with any valuable currency, success is believed to be in limited supply. We wrongly assume that success is an unusual outcome. We falsely convince ourselves that success is far from reach and limited to a select few. It's not.

This is why I chose to name this book *Success Freak*. We are all freaks and we don't even know it. And by freak, I mean "success" freak. The definition of "freak" is a "very unusual and unexpected event or situation" or refers to a person with something strikingly unusual about their behavior. Everyone can become a freak of success and here's why: because we are ALREADY wired for success. It's an energy source that simply must be rediscovered, channeled and unleashed; we just need to know HOW. This is the journey we are about to take together.

As a part of this journey, I want to invite you to consider a more holistic, lasting, and personally-relevant definition of what constitutes success; a definition that will profoundly change you and your outlook on life, a sort of visual cue you maintain while you passionately climb your personal ladder. To do so, we should open our minds to a new perspective that defies the social norm.

By reading this book and, therefore, investing in yourself,

you are taking your first critical step toward becoming YOUR own astonishing success story. This is no ordinary expedition. As with any lifechanging endeavor, we must have the resolve to grab life with our own hands. We must leave old habits, old ways of thinking, and never look back.

Are you ready?

Successful people are willing to commit to a regimen of effortful behaviors designed to get them to move forward, step by step, away from comfortable mediocrity of the status quo. They eagerly take on whatever new challenge life throws at them and, as you know, there are plenty of those out there. Every accomplishment gets them closer to their goal. These highly-motivated individuals can sample the sweet, addictive, and exhilarating taste of success. They want more, so they keep working tirelessly and continue achieving. And they do, day after day, energized by small victories.

Consider, what made it possible for the Wright Brothers to achieve man's historic quest to change air travel—discovering one of the greatest technical feats of all time? Or what made it possible for Edward Jenner and Louis Pasteur to successfully develop vaccines that would save the lives of millions, and thus, one of the most extraordinary medical achievements of the twentieth century? The greatest accomplishments in human history, from flying to the moon, to conquering Mt. Everest, to mapping the human genome, are overwhelming testaments to the power of the human spirit and our instinctive thirst for advancement and success. There is no doubt, it's in our DNA.

Now what? These are well-known accomplishments by what appear to be super-humans. What does it mean to you and me, ordinary mortals? When I speak of unleashing the Success Freak in you—this extreme, wild form of individual success—

I am not only talking about extraordinary human achievements as you find them in textbooks or the *Guinness World Records*. I am speaking to everyday personal or professional achievements—those we realize when we set our minds and hearts to pursue what we love, take chances on, and reach our goals doing whatever it takes.

You don't need to be a superhero born with superpowers to propel yourself forward and blast through life. Being successful is within everyone's reach, and it's not as hard as it seems—but it will take effort. It takes heart and brains, as well as faith, courage, and determination to confront your own truths and pursue your wildest ambitions. It will also require discipline. See, success is not a gift we receive, it's an opportunity we seize. We must look for it, as it will not look for us.

DON'T BE TOO HARD ON YOURSELF, OTHERS WILL DO THAT FOR YOU

We all aspire to live fulfilling lives, full of choices about how we want to spend our time. Yet life often takes a detour. Sure, we can be slowed down. We can even be thrown off course, but we can also be challenged to overcome new obstacles when we least expect them. Most people end a busy day with a heavy heart, often going to bed disillusioned. Time flies and dreams remain unfulfilled. People often sense that their choices are limited, and their options are evaporating. They are driving fast and furious, but somehow, along the way, they miss that critical turn, running out of gas or crashing into a wall of indifference and complacency. Uncertainty settles in and fears of failure and rejection spread like a virus. Although they are unhappy with their situation, they no longer have the appetite to step outside of their comfort zone, turning the sweet hope of success sour with overwhelming doubts. Have you ever felt that way?

We all do, at some point in our life. This is part of the ride to some degree, and perhaps we accept it too readily. If you are growing afraid of making changes or moving in a new direction, then you know what I'm talking about. You whisper to yourself: *"If only I had more time!"*, *"If only someone guided me through this maze that is life!"* or *"If only I had known with absolute certainty what path to take!"* Many people look back at their life and wish they had done more.

Don't doubt yourself or be too hard on yourself—more importantly, don't settle. We cannot be defeated if we pursue purposeful lives and commit ourselves to acting with love, passion, and resolve. Soon, you will realize that the world is too small for those who dream big. Today, let's go ahead and dream big. This book will guide you on how to transform your life as it is today and unleash the amazing potential that, yes, already lies within you. Like a switch that must be turned on, this book may simply be the lever you've been looking for.

No matter how we were raised, what values we were taught during childhood, what qualities we developed, or what our personal circumstances might be, we are all aspiring to reach goals that define us as accomplished human beings. We are motivated to see it through.

Success is achieved, not inherited. Thankfully, most of us are willing to invest time, energy, and resources to set ourselves on the path to a successful outcome. Yet we often take too much and give too little. Pretty obvious, yet this is a powerful idea. Here's some good news: This is about to change.

REVEALING THE CONCEALED
CODE OF SUCCESS

Until you know what you want, not much can be accomplished. You have to ask yourself why you want it, and are you are willing to do something about it? Are you committed to work at it incredibly hard, no matter the obstacles? You may wonder: How do we get there? Can behavioral science, books, articles, workshops and other resources help us achieve success, or determine key skills required to be successful? How do we reproduce the priceless recipe for success, so we can all live successful lives? Here lies the perplexing beauty of a conversation that started in the past century. How do we do it? Motivational speakers have offered words of wisdom about achievement, often based on intuitive ideas, rehashed universal truths, and common sense that have been around for centuries.

Our culture celebrates success, and then goes out to dissect and study its origin so others can replicate it, looking to satisfy our burning thirst for practical solutions. You hear people often refer to the "secrets of success" because well, there is no exact science behind it. If there were, it wouldn't be a secret any more, would it?

Instead, I like to think about it as a code that must be deciphered. The ingredients of success lie in every one of us, dormant at times, but, as muscle memory, can be awakened with the right skills. Success is a bit like a puzzle: you already have all the pieces, and now you just need to assemble them the right way. Where do you start?

Too few people know what it takes to get there. They lack the skills and savoir faire that embodies effective people and urges them to question the assumptions that shape their lives.

There are too many "internal interferences," as neuroscientists call them, such as fear, stress, doubts, and nervousness that get in the way and prevent us from unlocking our full potential. This book will undoubtedly change that for you, too.

Success Freak is first and foremost a mindset, a renewed sense of confidence, no matter what your disposition might be. *Success Freak* is also a practical playbook with a set of specific skills, no matter your education or professional background, that must be put into use daily. Being human is having the capacity to transform ourselves and to create the world that we really want. We may hope for more favorable winds. But now is our time to take a chance, acquire these skills and start sailing.

HOW WE SEE OURSELVES CHANGES US

The topic has never been so timely and socially relevant. We aspire to succeed—at home, at school, at work, and in every facet of our lives. The pressure has never been greater, either—from parents, family members, employers, teachers, friends, coaches. Success is another powerful lens on how we see ourselves and others. It's also how we begin the process of changing ourselves. Are we justified in desiring to develop and exercise new life-changing skills? Absolutely.

Success is our pathway to a bright, exciting future. It's a label we casually apply to the many slices of our busy lives—professionally, personally, physically, emotionally, intellectually, and even spiritually—and on which we reflect. To get started, we must ask ourselves:

Do I possess the necessary skills to set myself up for success?

Am I setting a clear path toward achieving those goals?

Am I confident enough that I can shape my own future?

Am I ready to overcome setbacks along the way?

How will I hold myself accountable?

These questions pave the path for us in the next few chapters. We are about to embark together on a journey that includes the following major stages:

OUR JOURNEY TOGETHER

YOU ARE HERE

STAGE A
I don't have the skills or know-how
LEARN THE 7 CRITICAL SKILLS TO SUCCESS

STAGE D
I'm not confident that I can do it
BUILD CONFIDENCE IN YOURSELF

STAGE E
I experience some setbacks but I stick to it
COMMIT YOURSELF AND OVERCOME CHALLENGES

YOU DID IT!

STAGE B
I want to start but don't know where
APPLY THE SKILLS YOU LEARNED

STAGE C
I see some initial progress but I'm not there yet
MEASURE YOUR PROGRESS AND CELEBRATE EARLY SUCCESSES

STAGE F
I reach my goals and I'm now the success freak I always wanted to be
ACCOMPLISH YOUR DREAMS AND SHARE WITH OTHERS

TIME TO UNLEASH THE SUCCESS FREAK IN YOU: A SEVEN-DAY CHALLENGE
To reach our destination, we will acquire new practical skills or refine and apply them. We all have busy lives and time is a currency in ever-dwindling supply. Admittedly, few of us have the luxury of sitting down for hours to

attend weeks-long workshops or read self-improvement books. How many books have you started reading, only to begin the entire book or a given chapter again, because you hardly remember what you last read? Chances are that you have a collection of books at home you never finished. You are not alone.

This book is different. This is precisely why I came up with a framework called the "Success Freak Seven Day Challenge." Here's how it works: You are invited to read this book in seven days, dedicating less than one hour per chapter during that one-week period. At the start of each chapter, you will see the estimated time for reading that chapter and for completing the exercise. One hour per day for a week should be a reasonable time commitment for anyone with a busy lifestyle. As you complete each chapter, you will discover an essential skill that you must develop (if you don't already have it) or strengthen (if you do). In each chapter, there are a handful of challenging questions to reflect on and answer at your convenience. It's then followed by seven recommended actions to take each day. In one week, you will have these critical skills.

You may wonder: why are seven and not four, ten, or even fifteen skills required to be well on your way to becoming successful? After years of secondary research and based on my extensive conversations and experience dealing with highly successful individuals in a variety of fields, I reached the following conclusion: despite the many potential skills one could acquire and build—many of which have been topics of excellent self-improvement books—there are only seven that are truly essential and are deal-breakers. In other words, you need the complete set to be successful. Here are the chapters and seven core skills to master:

- In **Chapter One (Day One, Skill One)**, you will learn how to create your own measurement of success rather than comparing yourself to others. This is the first skill to build.

- In **Chapter Two (Day Two, Skill Two)**, you will explore ways to think and act differently. Instead of conforming to standards that are not your own, you'll learn how to live by your own rules.

- In **Chapter Three (Day Three, Skill Three)**, you'll discover how some failures are not only necessary, they are essential to strengthening your character.

- In **Chapter Four (Day Four, Skill Four)**, you will learn to balance the need for reflection with the necessity of getting things done.

- In **Chapter Five (Day Five, Skill Five)**, you will learn how to accomplish more by managing your time more effectively, turning time into a powerful asset, instead of a scarce commodity.

- In **Chapter Six (Day Six, Skill Six)**, you will explore how resilience is essential to seeing your ambitions through and learn the virtue of never giving up.

- In **Chapter Seven (Day Seven, Skill Seven)**, you'll discover what it means to think and live boldly, and how to pursue a life of passion and purpose. This is the last skill to master.

Each chapter includes important insights, inspiring stories and anecdotes that bring these seven skills to life. At the end of each chapter, you will find:

» Easy-to-carry-out **exercises**—thought-provoking questions—designed to make you reflect on how those take aways apply to you.

» An **action plan**—composed of seven specific activities—to immediately apply what you just learned into everyday practice.

In a short period of time, using all of these resources, you will have acquired everything you need to effectively turn your life around and "kick ass." You can't win fights you don't take on, but if you commit to embracing these seven skills, you'll be well on your way to winning that fight and drastically changing your life for the better.

LET'S GET STARTED!
The most important investment you can make is in yourself. So please join me.

The journey might be uncomfortable at times and it will be challenging. It will likely force you to question what's truly important to you or reexamine old habits, but it will open your mind to groundbreaking opportunities, day in and day out, to test and apply your newly developed skills.

Your life is about to take off like a rocket; fasten your seat belt and get ready! You are about to become an unstoppable force of resolve and determination: nothing less than the Success Freak you were always meant to be.

START HERE

DAY 1 CREATE YOUR OWN PERSONAL MEASUREMENT OF SUCCESS

DAY 2 THINK AND ACT DIFFERENTLY, LIVING BY YOUR OWN RULES

BE OBSESSIVELY OUTCOME-ORIENTED **DAY 4**

DAY 3 LEARN TO FAIL SMART AND STRENGTHEN YOUR CHARACTER

DAY 5 ACCOMPLISH MORE BY MASTERING THE EFFECTIVE USE OF TIME

SEVEN STEPS

to kicking ass

IN LIFE

DAY 6 DEMONSTRATE UNMATCHED DEDICATION AND RESILIENCE

DAY 7 PURSUE A LIFE OF BURNING PASSION AND PURPOSE

YOU DID IT!

DAY ONE, SKILL ONE

"There is only one success — to be able to spend your life in your own way."

CHRISTOPHER MORLEY
Journalist, Novelist & Poet

Permission to reproduce from Christopher Morley's WHERE THE BLUE BEGINS granted by the Christopher Morley Literary Estate

CHAPTER ONE

YOU ARE NOT THE BOSS OF ME

DAY ONE, SKILL ONE

Create your own personal measurement of success

ESTIMATED READING TIME: THIRTY MINUTES
ESTIMATED EXERCISE TIME: FIFTEEN MINUTES

 What do a young boy with a lightning bolt-shaped scar on his forehead, pebbles in a jar, and the North Star shining above our heads have in common? More than meets the eye, actually. Together, they hold the keys to understanding what "being successful" really means, deep down, for each one of us personally. Intrigued? Good. Let me explain further.

In the month of February 2004, something quite remarkable happened that would change our understanding of what's possible. The leading magazine, *Forbes*, named the first person in the world to become a billionaire by writing books. That's right. Not by building software, like self-made multi-billionaires Bill Gates and Larry Ellison, or in investing, like Warren Buffett and Michael Bloomberg, but rather by writing fiction books, essentially aimed at young readers. Have you ever read a *Harry Potter* book, or seen one of the movies? Well, I haven't escaped her reach either. My kids would make me go to see the movies in hopes of one day enrolling at Hogwarts School of Witchcraft and Wizardry.

The books have attracted a wide adult and youth audience in historically unprecedented ways. With the flick of a magic wand, the *Harry Potter* series, now the most celebrated book series of modern times, sold over 500 million copies in over fifty-five languages. That's right, half a billion copies worldwide and growing strong. That's enough books for one in every fourteen individuals in the world to get their hands on these novels.

The celebrity author could not have imagined the influence her youthful imagination would have. Frankly, no one did. The books have also been the basis for a series of blockbuster movies, which have done incredibly well at the box office. As of 2015, the Harry Potter film franchise is the second-highest-grossing film franchise of all time, with the eight released films grossing more than $7.7 billion worldwide. By all standards, this is an extraordinary commercial success story.

ACCEPT THAT $650 MILLION WON'T MAKE YOU SUCCESSFUL, OR HAPPY, EITHER

$6.5 million won't make you successful or happy either. Neither would $65 million. Unless, of course, all you care about is having significant wealth. This statement may perhaps sound crazy to you. Let me ask you this then: Would you personally consider J.K. Rowling, the novelist and creator of the Harry Potter phenomenon, a success story? Here are a few more reference points before you answer this somewhat obvious question: In 2017, Rowling's fortune was estimated at $650 million (after donating approximately $150 million over time to charities, according to *Forbes*). In 2004, at age thirty-eight, she was of the youngest people and the only British female on *Forbes'* billionaire list. She has received countless awards and honorary degrees from top universities, including Harvard University, for whom she spoke at the 2008 commencement ceremony. She has been named as one of the most powerful women in the United Kingdom by leading magazines. So far, so good, right?

However, it wasn't smooth sailing the entire way. That story didn't just happen out of sheer luck. The distinguished author, screenwriter, and film producer finished her first manuscript for *Harry Potter* on an old manual typewriter in 1995, before submitting it to twelve publishing houses, all of which ended up rejecting it. Every single one turned it down without hesitation. It was only a year later that a brave publishing house would give the modest researcher and bilingual secretary a chance to get published and, by doing so, change history. Yet, before the Harry Potter success, J.K. Rowling lived in relative poverty for years. She also got divorced and became jobless at one point with a dependent child. She lost her mother who suffered from multiple sclerosis. Rowling was once diagnosed with clinical depression and even contemplated suicide at one point in her life.

Now, let's go back to the question at hand: How do you think J.K. Rowling defines her own success? Is it her artistic accomplishments, or her actual writing? Is it the satisfaction of knowing that she overcame so much in her life to get to where she is now? Is it her notoriety as a recognized, widely awarded author, despite the initial rejections? Or is it buying a nineteenth century house in Kensington, West London, for £4.5 million and being able to own her other estates after overcoming painful poverty? Is her life today what she imagined it would be? Are her colossal commercial achievements and financial results tangible insights into her amazing success? It's hard to say.

FORTUNE IS NEVER THE SIGN OF A SUCCESSFUL LIFE OR A MEANINGFUL MEASURE OF SUCCESS.

Would it help you in your assessment if I told you that Rowling established a trust to combat poverty and social inequality, support one-parent families, and fund multiple sclerosis research efforts? Or that the British philanthropist has also contributed money and support for many non-profit foundations and organizations seeking to help people in need? Which of these accomplishments are the most meaningful to her? How many of her personal goals has she been able to realize? Is Rowling a success in your eyes, and if so, why?

Based on common standards, most people would say so, absolutely. To me, J.K. Rowling is a Success Freak. Look at all she did on her own, despite having so little. Imagine the life she must have now compared to where she started.

But realistically, does it matter what you and I think about her success? It's easy to throw big numbers, like her net worth, and jump to conclusions. We both know that the only person who can accurately answer this intricate question is J.K. Rowling, herself. The lesson here is clear: success is always personal, no matter what others might think.

LOOK BEYOND THE OBVIOUS OR THE NORM
Let's face it, we tend to look up to celebrities who are front and center in our ever-expanding portfolio of media channels, from magazine covers to TV shows, capturing our undivided attention. These days, fame, or the pursuit of popularity, goes far beyond the few chosen ones who have reached the status of mega stars. Celebrity is also of utmost value in our social media universe, where YouTube, Facebook, Snapchat, and Instagram followers by the millions often translate "likes" into social status.

That's certainly the case for Italian-born Chiara Ferragni who ranked first on the *Forbes* list of most powerful fashion influencers in late 2017. As of January 2019, ten years after starting her fashion blog, the Italian influencer and fashion businesswoman reached sixteen million followers, collaborating with Gucci and other iconic brands.

Whether it's in fashion, travel, fitness, beauty, entertainment, or food, there are hundreds of new iconic personalities using their skills to build large social media audiences. In that world, reach (how many people are following you) and engagement (how many people "like" your posts or comment on them) are the metrics that determine one's economic value in the digital sphere.

These grassroots online celebrities, in desperate pursuit of avid followers and fans, quickly become influencers and connectors within their social community of choice. They also attract big advertising budgets from brands looking to capitalize on them and their ever-growing circles. Enabled by digital technology, social influence is the new organic way to chase fame and premier status. We feel an exhilarating sense of importance and accomplishment when we reach a certain level of popularity. It's an exciting opportunity to build our egos and shine in the world.

Of course, we also look up to those who are the wealthiest and have acquired massive capital or power. Due to their wealth and overall influence, they become de facto role models and a source of envy and admiration. After all, we have always celebrated entrepreneurial personalities and earth-shaking commercial successes like self-made media titan Oprah Winfrey, and business magnate and innovator Elon Musk. Although the question is obvious: are they truly role models and desirable benchmarks for your definition of success?

The expression, "Some people are so poor, all they have is money" speaks well to our understanding of the limitations of wealth as the sole measure of success. As in J.K. Rowling's case, the definition is far from being so clear.

In the 2018 documentary *Generation Wealth*, the mindless yet popular (sometimes obsessive) pursuit of materialism, celebrity culture, and social status—at any cost—is examined, pointing out its potentially disastrous implications. Shouldn't we welcome a definition of success that incorporates a much broader range of accomplishments?

Even Steve Jobs, the legendary co-founder and iconic CEO of Apple, Inc., said that being the richest man didn't matter to him… even if you are the richest man in the cemetery. For him, success was ending the day knowing that he accomplished something wonderful or remarkable. Reflect on that for a second: What is that thing you've done and consider to be "remarkable" in your life, but might not make you wealthy?

Is wealth over-rated? Yes and no, but mostly yes. A 2010 psychological and cognitive sciences study published in the *Proceedings of the National Academy of Sciences* concluded that high income (above $75,000 per year) improves evaluation of life but not emotional well-being. Surely, one's socioeconomic status and access to adequate income have a reasonable impact on overall well-being, objectively and subjectively. However, only health and emotional well-being are essential to being and feeling truly successful. Wealth and materialistic drive, despite common beliefs, rarely lead to satisfaction in life. This is not just an opinion. Research indicates that winning the lottery, for example, doesn't make people happier in the long term. A study by the American Psychological Association compared lottery winners and paralyzed accident victims and concluded that lottery winners were not happier than accident victims and took significantly less pleasure from a series of mundane events. At the risk of oversimplifying this study, these findings support the notion that happiness is relative, and that wealth is indeed over-rated.

Yet success has always been synonymous with financial wealth, influence, and status. *The Merriam-Webster Dictionary*[1] defines it as "attainment of wealth, favor, or eminence." We can all agree that this definition seems awfully narrow and inadequate to capture such a broad concept. To make the point, we've all heard the names of famous and wealthy individuals who struggled to find peaceful, purposeful lives, and ultimately died too soon. Judging their lives based on our simple and

---

1   By Permission. From Merriam-Webster.com ©2019 by Merriam-Webster, Inc. https://www.merriam-webster.com/dictionary/success]

narrow cultural standards, everything would point to a group of highly "successful" individuals who were living their dreams and passions to the fullest. To the naked eye, their numerous accomplishments, their extraordinary fame and fortune, would make them successful role models and inspiring examples. Yet their tragic endings suggest that much of their personal or professional disappointments and struggles, including mental illness, and—one can assume—personal definition of success, was simply invisible to the public eye.

Somehow, we find it difficult to comprehend that these talented individuals fell short of finding the sort of peace and fulfillment you would expect from successful individuals who have so many vast resources and opportunities within their reach. These extreme, yet poignant, examples are another way to make an important point about what success is, and equally important, what it is not. Fame and fortune are far over-rated as success metrics. It doesn't speak to what someone might value most and might be painfully lacking to the point of despair.

To gain some insight into the social metrics of success per-ception, the CEO and co-founder of the social media bench-marking company, Unmetric, Inc., analyzed 2,000 editorial obituaries over a nearly two-year period using natural language processing to understand what life achievements would be celebrated. What do you think he found? The words "film," "theatre," "music," and "dance" represented over forty percent of words used, reinforcing that many life achievements are coming from non-famous individuals in interest categories that have little to do with financial wealth. Are you surprised? Let's put it another way: If you had the opportunity to write your own obituary, what would you say? Like you, I found the answer to that question to be eye-opening.

Why are societal values like wealth and fame so prevalent in our culture? Why are we struggling to define success for ourselves or getting so much resistance from those around us? If we defined our own success measures, wouldn't we be much happier than we are?

Let's look at this from another angle. According to the US Census Bureau, in 2015 nearly nine out of ten adults (eighty-eight percent) had at least a high school diploma or GED, compared to only one quarter who had completed high school in 1940. Nearly one in three adults (thirty-three percent) held a bachelor's degree or higher, compared to five percent in 1940. The United States has always benefited from being a world economic leader. So, in theory, more people in the US have access to education, a favorable economic environment, and endless opportunities. Yet the happiness score—which includes variables like GDP per capita, social support, life expectancy, freedom to make life choices, etc.—ranks the United States as thirteenth on its list of 155 countries, far below where you would expect to see it. Sadly, it continues to decline. In 2007, the US ranked third among the OECD (The Organization for Economic Co-operation and Development) countries. In 2016, it came in nineteenth.

I won't go into the complex ways we measure "happiness," or why Costa Rica, Israel, or even Iceland outperform what many consider to be the greatest country in the world, but subsequent analyses point to a social crisis and a general malaise among new generations in this country. Clearly there are many contributing factors that go beyond the focus of this book. However, the lack of self-realization is a major contributor to the low ranking of the United States and a much-needed topic of research and debate.

Even the billionaire and business magnate Warren Buffett, one of the richest people in the world, claims that his measure of success is not his prosperity and vast wealth, but asks if the people you care about the most love you back. Do they love you back unconditionally? It's a healthy perspective. Fame and fortune are not necessarily bad to have, as long as they are not considered the end goal, and can also be used to do good. For example, having some fame allows you a sort of "giant" microphone as an opportunity to spread your message to the masses. Wealth also allows you to be philanthropic, supporting others in greater need.

HAPPINESS IS THE TRUE AND ONLY RELEVANT INDEX OF SUCCESS.

It's important to stay away from clichés and broad strokes here, no matter how tempting, because the meaning of "life" and "success" are different for every individual. The concept of success itself is first and foremost personal at the core. However, here is what's certain: we must look beyond fame and fortune, look beyond cultural norms—or what may seem obvious at first. Consider what brings you true, lasting happiness.

"DON'T ASK IF YOUR DREAMS ARE CRAZY; ASK IF THEY'RE CRAZY ENOUGH"

This is something quite personal to me. I started my humble journey towards personal achievements as a young Frenchman who immigrated to the United States over twenty years ago. I first came to the USA to study, and then pursued a rewarding career in advertising. This led me to professional opportunities working for the largest brands in the world, including global leadership roles at software giant Microsoft, and payment titan Visa.

When I moved to the United States, I spoke very little English. I furiously wrote down words I learned on random pieces of paper during the day, which were then organized alphabetically on the walls of my tiny dorm room in the hills of downtown San Francisco. I was learning day after day the meaning of every word I saw and heard. My father, a self-made man born in the west coast of France, had always admired the entrepreneurial culture of the United States. He instilled in me his contagious passion before passing away in my late teen years, due to health problems. What he didn't pass on to me was knowledge of the English language. Like many busy French men before him, speaking English was never high on his priority list. I had the opportunity to travel to the United States as a child, but my understanding of American culture came mostly from its popular music, movies, and iconic brands.

I was studying my way into the land of opportunity, throwing myself into a completely foreign culture and learning a new language. I was experiencing the American dream as a foreign student in a place that not only seemed to welcome, but also generously reward, hard work and risk-taking. I loved every minute of it. This is the same dream that encouraged immigrants like Jewish Ukrainian programmer Jan Koum, CEO and co-founder of the mobile messaging application WhatsApp, to pack his bags and pursue his version of the American dream. Do Wong Chan moved to the US from Korea to pursue his goals, becoming the co-founder and CEO of retail phenomenon Forever 21. There are thousands of other outstanding success stories in science, sports, and the arts that don't get the same public spotlight. Yet those are testaments to the bright light the United States still shines in the world for anyone willing to go after their wildest ambitions. If your dreams are crazy, this is the ideal place to see them through.

I would eventually land my first job working for a software company in Seattle, Washington. I was in good company, shoulder-to-shoulder not only with peers in my professional field, but also millions of other highly-motivated individuals! I learned so much through my journey. It not only shaped my perspective in life, but it gave me a deeper understanding of what real success meant. I was privileged to hold leadership positions for over a decade at some of the most respected companies in the world before starting my own software company with two friends of mine in the backyards of Microsoft and Amazon. All of which could have been perceived as unattainable when I had only a French passport in my pocket and an accent thicker than the clouds in Seattle on a winter day (I should know—I've lived in Seattle for over twenty years). I could have settled for realistic dreams, enjoying the comfort of living in the same country I was born or pursue a career in my native language. Yet, accepting my circumstances, learning and applying myself day in and day out, choosing crazy dreams for myself, I managed to grow professionally and personally. I ultimately became a Success Freak on my own terms.

We all have a story of our own. We all have unique circumstances that led us to where we are in life. Let me ask you this: Are you thinking big and bold enough? Are your dreams crazy enough? Are you pursuing them?

DEFINE SUCCESS FOR YOURSELF— AND FOR YOURSELF ONLY

If success is indeed personal to each one of us, how do we define it? How would we define an achievement of a lifetime? How do we overcome our social predispositions to focus on fame and wealth? Let's be frank: we grow up accustomed to having those around us define success for us. Our society provides clear success criteria that are difficult for anyone to ignore, no matter how hard we try. We reward good students, commend well-behaved children, encourage hard workers, acknowledge good neighbors, celebrate those who meet or exceed our expectations, and, ultimately, admire those who have secured great fortunes or made a name for themselves.

These criteria have been assimilated by most people from a young age, and we accept them at face value and it easily becomes a frame of reference for everyone. Pop culture and mass media contribute to reinforcing these as the most valuable proxies to make that determination for us. Subdued and partially numb from the constant barrage of cultural reference points, we just go along. It's hard to tune out and stay grounded. There are many respectable professions that will never get much media attention or even the biggest house in town. Yet, this success is nothing more than a view into our own world. The world doesn't define our view of success, we do. Success becomes our version of a world we want to live and thrive in—as it should. In the end, this broad and well-accepted definition of success in today's society fails to acknowledge the unique aspirations and desire of every individual. We are unique and, because we have different values and perspectives, we may see success where others see failure. We may also see failures where others see success.

> "To different minds, the same world is a hell, and a heaven."
>
> RALPH WALDO EMERSON
> *American essayist, lecturer, and poet*

How do we escape these overwhelming cultural biases? It all starts with a clear, individual definition of what success is. However, few can articulate what true success means to them. It's like a muscle we never trained or didn't train the right way. When it's time to answer that essential question, we feel greatly challenged. We ask ourselves:

- Am I clear about what I set out to accomplish?

- How satisfied am I with the direction of my life today?

- Is the opinion of others an important part of how I see the world?

- Is my purpose aligned with my everyday efforts?

- Am I making a difference in someone else's life and/or my own? Do I feel tremendous satisfaction from it?

- How will I know if I successfully reach my goals?

In the case of entrepreneur Adam Lowry, personal success was about creating a new type of cleaning product that didn't contain harsh chemicals or toxic ingredients. This is what real success was for the former climate scientist who started Method with a childhood friend, Eric Ryan, maxing out credit cards and borrowing money from family and friends. Method became one of the fastest-growing private companies in America, selling hundreds of products ranging from hand soaps to bathroom cleaners. Adam and Eric's definition of success is happy, healthy homes where "potentially toxic chemicals don't lurk beneath your sinks or lie in wait on your surfaces—homes where clean doesn't come with eye-watering, breath-holding side effects." Poisoning is the leading cause of injury-related death in the United States. According to the American Association of Poison Control, as many as 2.2 million individuals come in contact with all kinds of dangerous or potentially dangerous substances including cleaning products.

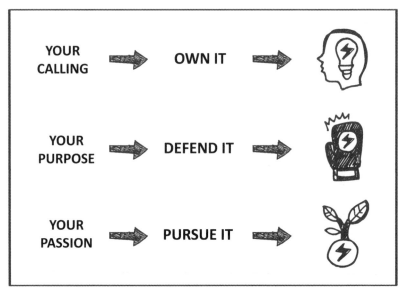

For Adam and Eric, saving a life might be their own and very personal definition of success. What is yours? This personal agenda is the burning candle inside you that can never rest. It doesn't get any more personal than this. Find and own your calling. When you know your purpose, defend it at all costs. Pursue your passion relentlessly as it is your most valued possession.

However, we often don't know enough about ourselves to reach that understanding with absolute certainty. We feel that we are destined for something of significance, but we find ourselves trapped in life circumstances. We have jobs that we need. We have bills to pay, mouths to feed. We are chained to many obligations, duties, responsibilities. We have lives others have dreamt for us, defined for us, maybe even passed on to us. That is not personal success. That's inherited social norm and paralysis.

WHETHER IN DOUBT OR PAIN,
LISTEN TO YOUR INNER VOICE
There is hope: You don't have to get lost before you can find yourself. Are you listening to your inner voice when life challenges you? You know, that voice inside your head and your heart that tells you to go right or to go left, to jump in or step back? It's always there. Every dream, every goal, every adventure and any real accomplishment in life begins and ends with faith in oneself. Never cease to believe in yourself. We too often feel that we are held captive in artificial jails we can't free ourselves from, at least until we finally come to understand what drives us, moves us, and what feels like second nature. You might call it your calling, life's purpose or passion. No matter what you call it, no matter how big or small it might be to others, it is YOURS.

My passion lies in giving people a chance at a life they may never know otherwise through knowledge that is inspiring and actionable. This is MY personal definition of success. This is why I enjoy writing about personal development, amplifying partnerships to create value, and conducting workshops for the world's largest companies. Over the

YOUR PASSION IS YOUR MOST VALUED POSSESSION. PROTECT IT FEROCIOUSLY.

course of a long career in business, I was offered many other compelling opportunities that would have led me to a very different place—not just geographically, but also professionally and emotionally. I was tempted. In the end, I listened to my inner voice. I followed my true passion.

Whatever yours is, own it, defend it, pursue it. Do not let others define your measure of success. As children inevitably reply when put under pressure to do something against their own will, "You are not the boss of me." We have all heard it, or even said it, in our own childhood. Children are simply defiant and take personal stands, as should any grown up trying to assert their personal definition of success. We must celebrate our desire for independent thinking.

We need to pay greater attention to our instincts and be satisfied when our inner voice tells us that we did our best. I had the opportunity to interview Martha Stewart—not the television personality and founder of Martha Stewart Living Omnimedia— the CEO of Soundzabound Music, which produces and licenses web based, copyright-safe audio for multimedia in education. (Though, she was once invited by *The Martha Stewart Show* to break a Guinness World Record by having the most people with the same first and last name together).

CHOOSE CAREFULLY IF YOU WANT TO BE A DRIVER OR A PASSENGER IN YOUR OWN LIFE.

The Martha Stewart I spoke to is one-of-a-kind, and nothing short of a remarkable success story. She listened to her inner voice and built a business from nothing, and watched it grow into the number one music company for schools in America. She shared with me these words of wisdom: "Define what success looks like to you. Be specific! Do you want a great marriage, a wonderful family, and a great job? I believe you can be successful in any relationship in life, and in any job you choose, if you will try to add value to the people and the company you are associated with. Wake up each morning with the thought of doing everything you do with excellence. You will find true joy in any project as long as you do it to the best of your ability!"

It reminded me of legendary basketball coach, John Wooden. With a track record that includes 620 victories and ten national titles, Wooden is one of the most admired coaches of all time. Wooden believed success is not a measure of performance competing with others, but rather a peace of mind. For him, it is about self-satisfaction and the knowledge that you did the absolute best you could.

What we admire in others already exist within. We are who we choose to become. We do our best and find great satisfaction in knowing that we did. When we doubt ourselves, when we get lost or side tracked, we simply need to pause and listen more carefully. As a life-saving compass, our inner voice always points us in the right direction. Listen.

FOCUS ON WHAT TRULY MATTERS

 I've heard this story told countless times, yet no one seems to know where the story originally comes from. This is probably one of the most inspirational stories about how to appropriately set priorities in our lives, determine what truly matters, and, ultimately, find personal success:

A teacher walks into a classroom and sets a glass jar on the table facing the students. He then pulls out a box of stones, each the size of an apple. He places the stones one by one in the glass jar until no more can fit. The teacher then asks the students if the jar is full. Everyone replies unequivocally with a "yes." After a short pause, the teacher then reaches under the table for another box now full of pebbles. He slowly pours the pebbles in the jar, allowing them to slip through the larger stones already in place. The teacher asks again if the jar is full. Now the students, who are starting to understand the lesson being taught, answer less categorically, "It is now!" The teacher now picks up a bag of sand hidden under the table and pours it into the jar, shaking it slightly. The sand slowly fills the empty spaces around the rocks and pebbles. Yet again, the teacher asks if the jar is full. Without any hesitation, the students reply, "Absolutely." The teacher once again reaches under the table, this time grabbing a bottle of water and pours it into the glass jar until it reaches the top. The students in look in awe at the professor for an explanation. The teacher went on to share with them an important life lesson:

> The rocks represent the most sizeable and meaningful things in your life—your spouse, your family, close friends, your health, your life dreams and ambitions. The pebbles are the other things in your life that are essential—your job, your relationships, your personal interests, and hobbies. The sand and water represent the most meaningless things of your life that fill your jar of time—watching TV, playing games, spending hours on social media. If you start over by adding sand and water first in the jar, followed by the pebbles, you soon realize that there is no more room for the stones. If we don't put all the larger stones in the jar first, we will never be able to fit all of them later.

BUILD YOUR OWN JAR OF LIFE

CHOOSE THE RIGHT MIX = YOUR OWN MEASURE OF SUCCESS

 **PRIORITY 1: ROCKS** (HEALTH, FAMILY, LOVED ONES, ETC.)

 PRIORITY 2: PEBBLES (JOB, CLOSE FRIENDS, ETC.)

 PRIORITY 3: SAND (SOCIAL LIFE, HOBBIES, ETC.)

 PRIORITY 4: WATER (WATCHING TV, PLAYING GAMES, ETC.)

The moral of this story? If you start by prioritizing things in your life, allowing you to dedicate more time and space for what's most important and purposeful to you personally, you are more likely to live a full life and be successful. Your purpose in life is the beginning and the end of your own story. Choose it and assemble it carefully, prioritizing what matters to you personally first.

STAND BY YOUR SUCCESS MEASURES AS IF YOUR LIFE DEPENDED ON IT

Being your own measure of success is easier said than done. How well do you know yourself? What defines YOU? Education, family, relationships, career? Think again. Our ability to say YES to our dreams says so much more about who we are.

There are many psychological and emotional obstacles that must be overcome to be able to define personal success. We must protect ourselves against those things and people in our lives that attempt to distract us, slow us down, or try to redirect us—steering us away from our core purpose. They will make you doubt and challenge you to change course. They will critique you and try to destabilize you. These pressures are real. We are greatly influenced by our environment and those around us and can be tempted to listen to others instead of relying on our personal instincts. It's only human.

As we saw in the jar of life story, if you fail to prioritize and let others decide for you, your life will be filled up with less important things and you won't be able to find room to fulfill your personal goals, find happiness, and be successful. This is something I practice daily: I am my biggest fan and my toughest critic. I set my own limits. I choose what goes in the jar. However, you cannot define personal success until you have reached a certain level of self-awareness about intrinsic motivations, faith in yourself, and a deep sense of purpose. Together, they make up your own treasure chest.

Taking responsibility for one's future is a worthy measure of success. Do you believe you can do anything? If not, why is that? How often are you held back by self-limiting beliefs or fears of asking tough questions about what truly matters in life? Ask yourself: is the source of your fear, that robs you of countless opportunities, realistic or rational? It often is not. A

DEFINE YOUR WORTH AND MEASURE YOURSELF BASED ON YOUR OWN EXPECTATIONS.

lifetime commitment always begins with one tiny brave step into the unknown. Once you get to the root of what success is deep down inside your own heart, it's easier to outline, get positive reinforcement from others, and see it through. You can now overcome your self-imposed limits. We are not perfect. We are not limited either. We are each a constant work in progress.

Spiritual teacher Deepak Chopra invites us to think about success as a matter of constant personal growth. In his book *The Seven Spiritual Laws of Success*, he calls success in life a sort of quest for happiness, a contant movement towards worthy goals.

Embrace what you already have. What you take for granted will eventually be taken. Seek worthy goals and don't let anything or anyone get in the way. Defend your success measures by pushing away those who challenge them or hold you back as you progress towards your goals. Fight and protect them as if your life depended on it, because it does.

PICK YOUR NORTH STAR AND SET YOURSELF FREE

Popularity and material possessions provide only short bursts of pleasure and happiness that cannot be sustained over time. Let's be real: by chasing the wrong things, you end up wasting a life that could be focused on pursuing what you love and what brings you peace. What you love becomes your North Star.

A North Star is the bright, visible star that looms directly overhead, keeping us on track. We all have one. It is what guided J.K. Rowling through her setbacks, what kept Adam and Eric of Method focused on what mattered most to them and how they define success. That North Star is what drove me from a small city in the Northwest part of France to the USA over two decades ago. It is what navigators used for centuries, both to find the direction of north, and to determine latitude. It is a focal point that helps us stay on the right path.

For most people, the true measure of success is living life to the fullest, doing things we love with people we cherish and treasure, pursuing our passions and dreams, giving back to the community, or simply helping those in need. Whatever it is, share your North Star and what it means to be successful with those around you. By communicating what success is to you, you won't convince them that their definition of success is wrong and that yours is right. On the contrary, we must embrace others and their own measures of success. By sharing what matters most to us, and where we are heading, we enable those around us to become a support system that can move us closer to our end goal more quickly.

Here is what Einstein could have said about success (the original quote was about everyone being a "genius" vs. being "stupid"): "Everyone is a success. But if you judge a fish by its ability to climb a tree, it will live its whole life believing that it is a failure." Success is meaningful only in the context in which we set our heart to do what we love most. In the end, personal success is, well, very personal. Come up with your own definition and be your own judge. Set yourself free.

CONSIDER THIS EXERCISE TO COMPLETE THIS CHAPTER.
WRITE DOWN ANSWERS TO THE
FOLLOWING QUESTIONS:

1. Can you name two or three of your favorite role models who are neither wealthy or famous? Please list what you admire most about them.

_____

_____

_____

_____

_____

2. What is the one thing you hope to accomplish in life that will make you most proud, and how would you measure it?

_____

_____

_____

_____

_____

_____

3. Do you believe those around you – spouse, parents, friends – consider you to be successful? How do their opinions of you realistically impact your own perception of how successful you are?

_____

_____

_____

_____

_____

_____

_____

_____

4. How do you handle internal conflicts when your inner voice and those around you differ on how you measure success?

_____

_____

_____

_____

_____

_____

5. Please list the activities for which you feel the greatest sense of personal fulfillment and that also move you closer to your North Star. Do you consistently prioritize them?

_____

_____

_____

_____

_____

DAY ONE, SKILL ONE
ACTION PLAN

Now that you have completed the exercise section and have reflected on ways
you can build this new skill, it's time to act. Here are seven specific actions
you must take to immediately apply what you've learned in this chapter:

CHALLENGE ONE:
CREATE YOUR OWN PERSONAL MEASUREMENT OF SUCCESS

☐ Declare what success is to you. Think beyond fame, fortune
and other cultural clichés. Write your definition of success
down; hang it on your wall; set goals that inspire you. Set
yourself free.

☐ Stay true to yourself, no matter what. Resist outside pressures to
box you in or to measure yourself by others' expectations.

☐ Prioritize wisely and avoid distractions. Place the big rocks and
pebbles in your jar first and make time for what matters most.

☐ Surround yourself with like-minded individuals who are successful
on their own terms and encourage others to find their own path.

☐ Trust your instincts and, when in doubt, follow your inner voice.

☐ Don't hold back. Pursue what matters most to you and set realistic
milestones for what you aim to achieve.

☐ Tell others how you define your own success, not to challenge or
influence them, but to seek their undivided support.

DAY TWO, SKILL TWO

"Rules are made for people who aren't willing to make up their own."

CHUCK YEAGER
*former United States Air Force officer
& the first pilot to exceed the speed of sound*

Permission granted by Victoria Yeager. www.chuckyeager.com, Twitter @GenChuckYeager

2
THINK DIFFERENT

DAY TWO, SKILL TWO
Think and act differently, living by your own rules

ESTIMATED READING TIME: TWENTY-FOUR MINUTES
ESTIMATED EXERCISE TIME: FIFTEEN MINUTES

 The year is 1826. In a southern suburb of Cape Town, South Africa, a frail-looking Royal British Army surgeon conducted a procedure considered highly dangerous at the time, but necessary, given the severity of the patient's situation: a cesarean operation. It was the first one performed by anyone in the British Empire. Thankfully, the operation was successful, and both mother and child survived.

That day, Dr. James Barry became the first doctor in the entire British Empire to perform such a medical procedure—a remarkable accomplishment of bravery and defiance at the time. So, after spending an entire medical career in the British Army, it's surprising that James Barry's true identity remained a military secret for nearly a century. It wasn't until Barry's death at age seventy-six that the shocking secret was revealed to the public: at age twenty, Margaret Ann Bulkley changed her physical appearance and became James Barry. Bulkley would spend the next fifty-six years of her life pretending to be a man to practice what she loved and revolutionize medicine. What motivated her to impersonate the opposite gender? Back then, Bulkley quickly realized that only men could join medical schools and pursue this line of work, so the disguised doctor found a means to break the rules and pursue her dreams, despite the gender restrictions of nineteenth century society.

Margaret would dress like a man to enroll as a medical student in 1809, never revealing her identity to those around her for the rest of her life. She was vocal about her reviews, and often made enemies by criticizing local officials for the way they handled medical matters. She strongly believed in providing better food, sanitation, and proper medical care to those in need. She also held strict and unusually modern views about nutrition. You see, Bulkley, the disguised military surgeon, was defiant, and saw things differently than the people of her time. This is why her story is noteworthy more than ninety years later. Bulkley was a Success Freak. The world remembers those who are not scared of thinking and acting differently.

More recently, who could ever forget the unknown Chinese citizen who stood in protest in front of a tank at Tiananmen Square in 1989? Who could forget African American civil rights activist, Rosa Parks, refusing to relinquish her seat to a caucasian passenger on the bus she took on December 1, 1955? Or Mohandas Karamchand Gandhi's Salt March, which sparked a movement to fight for India's independence?

In the business world, how about Jeff Bezos' 1994 decision to create Amazon, now the largest Internet-based retailer in the world, having challenged the well-established and traditional brick and mortar books stores with a pioneering e-commerce offering? Or Stanford University students Larry Page and Sergey Brin daring to index some sixty million pages on the internet in late 1998—now one of the most influential brands in the world, Google? How about industry disruptors like Tesla, Uber, or Netflix? These acts of individual defiance, not only in medicine, politics, and business, but also in sports, art, and science, showed the world that almost anything could be looked at and thought through differently.

DO *NOT* ALWAYS DO AS YOU ARE TOLD
Let's be real. Our lives are made of countless rules and guardrails that surround us and keep us in check. At least, that's what we are told. We accept and follow the often inflexible and punitive rules set by the environment and society we live in. We obey our parents, we listen to teachers and coaches, we do as we are told by employers. We rightfully comply with international, federal, and local laws (that's a very good thing by the way): "do not text and drive," "do not litter," "do not cross," etc. We sign employment contracts, insurance policies, and financial agreements that govern what we can or cannot do. We also encounter many environments where authority is minimal to non-existent that still attempt to dictate what we can or cannot do.

Many of these are negotiable in nature, by the way, but we rarely dare to challenge or question the established order. Sometimes they are even meant to guide people, not impose rules. We learn to respect and follow the policies and guidelines set forth by—real or presumed—authority figures in pretty much every aspect of our lives for the most part.

However, in most places, the early signs of rebellion are often punished at a young age before they can spread like an undesirable virus. The choice is painfully simple: we must obey or be punished for our insubordination. Our disobedience and defiance are treated as death sentences. Facing these complications, we often choose the path of least resistance—a sort of survival instinct eventually prevails to keep us out of trouble. By following the rules around us, we hope to be accepted and rewarded for conforming so conscientiously. In some instances, laws keep our society from falling into pure anarchy and we must play our part in respecting those. However, following the elective rules set by others is unlikely to set us apart and open our minds to new opportunities.

This is what Australian comedian Luke Kidgell promotes in his show *You Don't Own Me* presenting that rules are made to be broken, except if they have significant consequences. His hilarious Facebook videos, featuring him breaking every possible rule posted at corner streets, local grocery stores he encounters ("12 items or less," "keep left," "return your trolley here," "no entry," etc.) have gone viral and been viewed by millions. The videos are per-

PLAYING BY YOUR OWN RULES IS THE MOST EFFECTIVE WAY TO SUCCEED IN LIFE.

fectly matched with the popular 1963 song, "You Don't Own Me," recorded by Lesley Gore, which tells a lover that he does not own her, that he is not to tell her what to do or what to say.

Life is way too short, and people are far too resourceful to have to blindly conform to excruciatingly narrow concepts and directions imposed on us by society. These excessive, unnecessary rulebooks paralyze and suffocate us. And in the end, when we do not set our own direction, someone happily does it for us—guaranteed.

DON'T JUST DO WHAT FEELS RIGHT, DO WHAT IS RIGHT
Humans are strange creatures of habit. I often ask myself: Why do we religiously conform

to societal or social pressure? You don't need to be an expert in sociology or modern psychology to realize that we are conditioned from childhood to conform. We are taught what is right and wrong. We experience peer pressure whenever we slightly drift from the center lane. We follow pre-established patterns that have been set to simplify our world. We are exposed to rules that are presumably in place to protect us and others. In uncertain situations, we look for instructions and guidance.

There have been many scientific studies and experiments on the topic of peer pressure to conform, and how it significantly influences our judgement and individuality. One particularly noteworthy experiment is named after the psychologist Stanley Milgram who created an electric shock generator with thirty switches. For the purpose of this test, each switch was marked in fifteen-volt increments, ranging from fifteen to 450 volts. Forty subjects were recruited to participate in what they were told would be an experiment about "memory and learning." The subjects were unaware of the fact that the generator was indeed phony and would only produce sounds when the switches were activated. The subjects were told that they would receive payment no matter what happened during the experiment. The instructor who guided the subjects in these experiments appeared as a sort of medical authority. The instructor told the subjects to activate a switch every time the learner, a presumed recruit like the subjects themselves, failed at guessing the answer to a question, and to increase in fifteen-volt increments as the failed guesses mounted. The learner was a disguised actor sitting in an adjacent room, strapped to a chair with electrodes attached to their body, slowly but surely expressing pain and discomfort as the voltage appeared to increase.

The real purpose of this experiment was to determine the

answer to the following question: For how long will someone continue to give shocks to another person if they are told to do so, even if they believe the receiver could be seriously hurt? As the test continued, the instructor would reassure the subject by telling them that they alone were responsible and could decide whether or not to comply with the experiment. The findings were astonishing: Although most subjects were uncomfortable doing it, all forty subjects obeyed up to 300 volts. And twenty-five of the forty subjects continued to complete the experiment and gave shocks until the maximum level of 450 volts was reached, clearly understanding the potentially lethal nature of the voltage.

Before the experiment, the researchers expected a single digit percentage of individuals would be likely to conform and cause such pain once instructed to do so. Still, a shocking sixty-five percent of test subjects continued giving shocks to the learner, showing the incredible obedience most people show towards authority, no matter the severity of the outcome. What would you have done in this environment?

Most people are willing to live by the rules set by others, even if those rules are potentially harmful to others or themselves. It shows that people are inclined to conform under pressure, and even become sympathetic to the oppressor as a psychological release and a survival mechanism.

The experiment was described in the 2012 documentary called *The Lottery of Birth* by directors Joshua van Praag and Raoul Martinez. The fascinating documentary, which establishes that the mind is the battleground of familial, educational, cultural, and professional forces that converge to determine who we are from birth, illustrates the danger of conformity. Fear of loss, and insecurity increase conformity.

This was brilliantly illustrated in a British reality show called

The Push on Netflix. *The Push* is a disturbing social experiment show led by "psychological illusionist" Derren Brown. In the show, Brown exposes the psychological secrets of obedience and social compliance. When confronted with authority, our instinct is to obey without question, even

LIVING BY YOUR OWN RULES IS LIBERATING.

to go as far as committing immoral acts. In less than one hour, Brown demonstrates that an average individual can be led to pushing someone off a ledge by social pressure.

A reasonable amount of conformity and adherence to rules is safe. We avoid conflicts, we stay in our comfort zone, we believe that we are less likely to fail, we don't get marginalized and perhaps more importantly, we feel accepted by others. Although this allows most people to function harmoniously with others, it's now time to carefully reexamine our thought process and decision making. Now, you know: success is the sworn enemy of conformity.

THINK DIFFERENTLY

Steve Jobs, the former CEO and founder of Apple, is undeniably an icon of successful entrepreneurship and one of the most admired business executives of the twenty-first century. Apple's story is illustrative of a company and leader that set its own rules, challenged the status quo, and ultimately built one of the most valued companies in the world. Apple's success is, without a doubt, the result of many talented individuals and several important ingredients. However, the key to its wild success lies in the company's ability to challenge the status quo, write its own rules, and glorify those who do.

From a brand perspective, Apple's impact on the technology, music, entertainment, smartphone, and mobile computing space is nothing short of remarkable. It seems that Apple never played by any rules but its own, defeating many of its competitors in the process. For example, Apple reinvented the high-end retail store experience with over-the-top shopping and customer services. Apple redefined what we knew as a smartphone with the launch of the iPhone; revolutionized music with the launch of the iPod; and challenged the mobile computing space with the introduction of the iPad. Apple turned its customers into brand advocates, drawing crowds of anxious customers waiting in line at Apple stores to get the newest product upgrade. In the past decade, the high-tech company has received countless innovation awards for its impressive track record of creating new business models and paving the way for breakthrough technology and consumer experiences.

There is no better or more impactful way of capturing this mindset than Apple's "Think Different" campaign that set the company apart, fueling years of commercial success. The advertising campaign was created in 1997 by Apple's agency of record, the Los Angeles office of advertising firm TBWA\Chiat\Day. The short commercial featured black-and-white footage of iconic twentieth century personalities from Albert Einstein, Bob Dylan, Richard Branson, Mahatma Gandhi, and others who have profoundly impacted our perspective and view of the world. The message—which celebrates rebels, agitators, activists, people who simply see things differently, are not fond of rules, and ultimately contribute to change—is now immortalized into pop culture. The spot ends with an inspirational message: Only those who are brave enough to think they can change the world are the ones who will actually do.

We may think that those who defy rules are simply crazy. However, by writing their own rules, they move us forward. They do not fear the uncharted, unscripted, unpaved world in front of them. We admire them as they seem to be self-driven, self-motivated, and to have a clear sense of purpose. They do not fear authority. They do not fear change. They do not fear the unknown. They willingly challenge the status quo and open our minds to new ways of thinking about life and how to approach it.

These success freaks are the ones who ultimately change not only their world, but the world around us.

KEEP CALM... BUT BREAK SOME RULES
Conformity is also the sworn enemy of creativity and personal expression. Be anyone you want to be. Are you a rule breaker, a mover and shaker, a trail blazer? These are buzz words perhaps. Our environment growing up plays a big part in whether we see rules as obstacles or necessary guideposts.

I experienced this firsthand in my youth back home. I was privileged to be raised in France where the concept of "critical thinking" and non-conformity is an intricate part of the educational system and way of life. The French are known to defy rules and challenge each other—a heritage acquired during the French Revolution of 1789 when the monarchy was overthrown.

It's hard to ignore its impact on French society and way

of life. Today, it manifests itself in a sort of social unrest with frequent strikes that immobilize the country and remain a symbol of individual freedom. Critical thinking encourages open-minded reflection and healthy skepticism, which might explain why going on a strike there is such a popular activity. If you frequently travel to France, you may despise it at

YOU WILL NEED RULES... TO BREAK THEM.

times. While hugely inconvenient for us world travelers, the idea of protesting and challenging the status quo contributed to a law being passed in the late 1930s mandating twelve days each year of paid vacation for French workers, a groundbreaking concept at the time. I guess the French just don't like to do as they are told. The French have learned the most valuable lesson over the past centuries: If you don't break the rules, the rules might ultimately break you.

Rest assured, you don't have to be French, or move to France, to be exposed to non-conformism. For some, family dynamics may have contributed to non-conformity, such as having been raised by parents who occasionally broke society's rules themselves, or who lived by their own constant defiance. It can also be a coach or mentor, even a friend, who influences us; the heroes in our lives who we look up to in difficult times, because they open our minds to new possibilities. They are the rebels, eccentrics, creators, objectors, innovators, dissidents, and non-conformists who challenge conventional wisdom and find innovative ways to solve problems. It's all around us if we pay attention. By watching these success freaks swim against the stream, we've learned from them that there are alternatives to excessive conformism and that rules can—and often should—be broken.

BE A PURPOSEFUL NON-CONFORMIST

Being a non-conformist without a purpose is a bit like arguing without a position. If you choose to argue, make sure you have a reasonable purpose in doing so or you are simply wasting time and energy. A strong purpose is the equivalent of a life GPS, steering you in the right direction, no matter the circumstances. Sir Richard Charles Nicholas Branson knows something about it. The international adventurer, English business magnate, investor and philanthropist is, by all means, the perfect specimen of a maverick who doesn't conform or believe in following rules.

His life story seems to be a textbook example of non-conformism. Despite dyslexia and poor academic records, Richard Branson founded Virgin Records in 1972 at the age of twenty-two, after starting his first venture (a magazine called *Student*) at age sixteen. The British, self-made man and serial entrepreneur would later launch Virgin Atlantic Airways, Virgin Mobile, Virgin America,

THINKING OUT OF THE BOX IS GOOD, GETTING RID OF THE BOX IS BETTER.

Virgin Fuels, and many other companies in retail, music, and transportation. His approach has been to purposefully disrupt existing industries by challenging how things are done, completely transforming these businesses.

In his book, *Like a Virgin: Secrets They Won't Teach You at Business School*, he writes: "Had I pursued my education long enough to learn all the conventional dos and don'ts of starting a business, I often wonder how different my life and career might have been."

His biographic work speaks to the entrepreneur's adverse relationship with the status quo and with following rules: *Losing My Virginity: How I've Survived, Had Fun, and Made a Fortune Doing Business My Way, Screw It, Let's Do It, Screw Business as Usual.*

SHAPE YOUR OWN VALUES AND IDEAS. THIS IS A GPS TO GUIDE YOU THROUGH LIFE.

Richard Branson is another great example of a success freak who challenges the status quo. Rules often get in the way of creativity. They suppress one's ability to think outside of the box. Thinking out of the box is good, but it's not good enough. Get rid of the box altogether, if you can, and trust your instincts. The popular expression, "Rules are meant to be broken" invites us to be less conformist and more critical thinkers.

Ask yourself, are some rules excessively rigid in my life today? Do they make sense, or do they seem counterintuitive and unnecessarily restrictive? If you conform, you won't prevail. Don't get me wrong, there are times when following rules makes sense and might serve your purpose better. Conformity itself is not intrinsically wrong or unjustifiable; there are times when both the risks and consequences are too great to justify conforming, and times when it is wiser to toe the line. We all enjoy the benefits of rules, regulations, and laws in many facets of our everyday lives that keep civilized society from falling into absolute chaos. Those are essential to providing a predictable and often productive environment for everyone. However, our desire and tendency to conform leads us to accept situations and environments that propel a life of contradiction, stress, and insecurity.

Success Freaks don't break rules for the sake of being different. They have a purpose. By breaking them, they are different. But what motivates their behavior is their end goal—not merely to be labeled as mavericks or non-conventional thinkers. In the end, you know that the opinions of others might influence you, but they should not dictate the decisions you make. Instead, your decisions should be dictated by your own rules.

WANT TO CHART YOUR OWN PATH? THEN DECLARE YOUR OWN RULES

How do you set your own rules? It seems easier said than done. To think and act differently, we must live by principles, values, and rules that are our own, and not those imposed or defined by others.

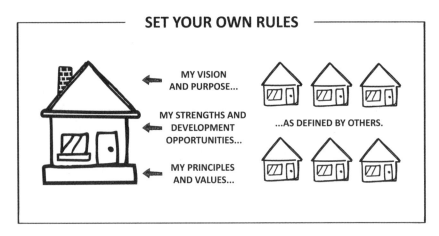

SET YOUR OWN RULES

MY VISION AND PURPOSE...

MY STRENGTHS AND DEVELOPMENT OPPORTUNITIES...

MY PRINCIPLES AND VALUES...

...AS DEFINED BY OTHERS.

Given the constant barrage of conventional rules society provides, it's challenging to put into practice. To set one's own rules, one must be able to exhibit these qualities:

My vision and purpose (internal vision): The only way to shape our destiny is to define it. Clarity of purpose is an intrinsic motivator for staying grounded and focused on the end goal. When we have a clear vision, we cannot be easily sidetracked, and others' opinions and guidelines do not have a profound impact on our own internal convictions and values. One example of an internal vision might be: "My parents were insistent that I take over our family real estate business, but I know deep down that my life's purpose is to promote understanding and compassion for special needs children through education and activism. My vision is to establish and run a non-profit organization that supports both children and struggling parents."

My strengths and development opportunities (self-awareness): Understanding one's strengths, development opportunities, and fears. When we reach a level of self-awareness, we can rationalize and articulate how we see others and the world. We know what principles we are comfortable following and what directions we must embrace to be true to ourselves. For example: "I work great in small, local groups or at managing deliverables on my own. However, my management often challenges me to take on a group leadership and coordination role, working with large distributed teams, which I don't feel I am ready to take on yet. I am quite good at inspiring people; however, I need to work on my listening skills."

 **My principles and values (code of conduct):** The ability to stay the course, not be overly-influenced by what others think of you, and the ability to live by your own principles and values. Those are essential muscles to propel us forward, set our own guidelines, and keep us from being thrown off course when things get really tough. For example: "I am one hundred percent committed to my goal and do not need encouragement or validation. I believe that success is only achievable when you set your own goals, monitor your progress regularly, and celebrate successes. I was told by my manager that I shouldn't apply for a promotion until I reached four years employment with the company, but I respectfully disagree. I am a hard worker. I believe in taking initiative and I think I am ready after two years of stellar performance. I have decided to give it a shot and apply, anyway."

This is a process I followed early on in my life. I was lucky to have the internal vision and clarity needed, regarding my purpose in life, to chart my own path. It takes a certain level of maturity and humility, and it took me much longer to accurately assess my strengths and accept my weaknesses.

Life experiences, such as a tragic loss, a professional setback, a trip abroad, or relocating to a new home may prompt this type of self-realization. As far as principles and values are concerned, being raised as a Catholic and living in France for the early part of my life equipped me with a strong foundation on which to build. My love for the American way of life and culture also contributed to the refinement of these principles and values over time. I learned to assess situations and make decisions that are in line with my personal code of conduct, no matter how difficult they might be. To me, that's integrity.

There is no better example than the French fashion designer, businesswoman, and founder of the internationally recognized Chanel brand to show one can live by his or her own principles and values. Gabrielle Bonheur "Coco" Chanel had the vision to liberate women from the constraints of the traditional "corseted silhouette."

BE CREATIVE ENOUGH TO THINK DIFFERENTLY. BE BRAVE ENOUGH TO ACT DIFFERENTLY.

She successfully popularized a more active, casual chic as the feminine standard of style in French high society. At the age of twelve, she was a very self-aware individual. After the death of her mother, she experienced a very frugal and disciplined upbringing at the orphanage convent of Aubazine. The talented couturière learned to sew there and realized early on that, in order to be of exceptional value to others, one must always be unique and stand out. The soon-to-be fashion phenomenon would come to define a set of principles and values that would guide her through difficult times, set her apart from other designers, and contribute to her remarkable accomplishments in her professional and social life. Coco Chanel knew the importance of setting her own rules.

LET YOUR CHARACTER SHAPE HOW YOU APPROACH LIFE

We spend too much time trying to conform to others' perceptions of us. We are unmistakably unique. Values, principles, and one's ability to set personal rules are inextricably intertwined. It takes character to identify these values and principles and put them into practice every day. In fact, the etymologic origin of the word "character" is from the Ancient Greek χαράσσω (kharássō, "I engrave"). When we show character, we approach the world with strength of mind, individuality, independent spirit, moral strength, and determination. Why does it matter? It takes character to have the courage and mindset to steer your life in a different direction than others might expect. No one else can determine our path in life. Yet it won't stop people from trying to tell us who we must become. When forging our own paths, we often go against the tide and encounter significant resistance in the process. We must be prepared to accept the consequences of living by our own rules, grounded by our values and principles.

Character can offer the internal compass required to validate our decisions without looking back. We must stop looking for outside approval of the life and the decisions we make, the values we want to emulate, or the rules by which we intend to play. By pressing forward with the certainty that we are making the right move, we can move faster, letting go of the distractions that come from trying to receive outside validation, or from society at large. Values and principles are what we must rely on when we lack the data to make decisions. We must follow our gut instincts and rely on them to press forward with conviction.

GET AMAZINGLY GOOD AT SAYING "NO"
Most people have a hard time saying "no." This is at the root of conformity and over-commitment. We say "yes" too much, even when we don't mean it. We want to be empathetic, accommodating, comforting, or reassuring. The desire to please and be agreeable comes naturally to us. We really feel like saying "no," but we end up saying "yes" to avoid hurting someone's feelings, letting them down, or creating unwanted tension or conflict in relationships that matter to us. I bet you can think of a couple of times in the past week where you walked away from a situation wanting to kick yourself in remorse: "Why didn't I simply say 'no?'" We don't realize how liberating it is to say "no," especially when there is a valid reason for it. The more we say "no," to things that are not a priority, the greater our ability to say "yes" to the things that matter to us. We must start saying "no" gracefully, kindly, and unapologetically to requests that do not fit into our personal goals and free ourselves up for the "yeses" that do.

The world needs more leaders to disrupt the status quo. If you are to successfully reach your goals, do not let fear stop you from thinking and acting outside the norm, or from making your own rules; dare to be different. We struggle when we are not ourselves and try to conform for the wrong reasons. In the end, we can change how we look and communicate, but we can't fully transform until we allow ourselves to reach our full potential by being our true selves.

Setting our own rules means setting ourselves free. Free to pursue what we love and what we believe matters; to tune out the noise, to embrace our inner voice. Once you set your own rules, you must stick to them, at least for a while.

EXERCISE #2

COMPLETE THIS EXERCISE TO FINISH THIS CHAPTER. WRITE
DOWN ANSWERS TO THE
FOLLOWING QUESTIONS:

1. What conventional thinking and principles do you wish you could
break away from to pursue your dreams?

2. What rules in your life are you conforming to, even though you feel
they are excessively restrictive and limiting?

3. Do you currently consider yourself a contrarian? List the negative
implications of living a life of conformity.

4. How would you handle the pressure of objections and/or rejections from those closest to you, if you refused to play by their rules?

5. What top values are essential to creating a new way of life in order to pursue your personal aspirations?

DAY TWO, SKILL TWO

ACTION PLAN

Now that you have completed the exercise section and have reflected on ways
you can build this new skill, it's time to act. Here are seven specific actions
you must take to immediately apply what you've learned in this chapter:

CHALLENGE TWO:
THINK AND ACT DIFFERENTLY, LIVE BY YOUR OWN RULES

☐ Identify key societal/cultural rules that currently hold you back
or make you conform to ideas that are not yours. Learn to
suppress them.

☐ Openly challenge the status quo in important aspects of your
life. Reexamine what led you to it and consider alternatives.

☐ Allow yourself room to think/act differently. Be rebellious.
Reject the most dangerous idea in the world: It has always been
done this way.

☐ Pick the road less traveled as needed. Conduct self-awareness and
stay true to your internal compass, even if you must travel alone.

☐ Articulate what principles/values must now guide your life and key
decisions. Make a list and review before making big decisions.

☐ Understand which rules in your life are negotiable and which
are not. Get amazingly good at saying "no" at least once per
day. Stay firm under pressure.

☐ Weren't you listening earlier? Ignore rules 1 through 6 and
come up with your own. Start thinking different now.

DAY THREE, SKILL THREE

"A ship in harbor is safe, but that is not what ships are built for."

JOHN AUGUSTUS SHEDD
American Author & Professor

SUCCESSFUL FAILURES

DAY THREE, SKILL THREE

Learn to fail smart and strengthen your character

ESTIMATED READING TIME: TWENTY MINUTES

ESTIMATED EXERCISE TIME: FIFTEEN MINUTES

 Do you sweat? Well, most people do, yet sweating is something we rarely look forward to as we don't want to stink or experience the unpleasant feeling. Instead, we tend to hide or suppress it as much as humanly possible. We are so conditioned to think that sweating is gross and undesirable—often associated with poor hygiene and care—that American families spent $4.5 billion in deodorant products in 2016, a twenty-three percent increase between 2011 and 2016, according to data from Euromonitor.

This personal care category, led by packaged good companies like Unilever and Procter & Gamble, is expected to grow sixteen percent by 2021, helping us reduce underarm irritation and fight odors with fragrances. We are bombarded with commercials that tell us how to stop excessive armpit sweating or how to control premature perspiration. We all remember the award-winning TV commercials, "The Man Your Man Could Smell Like," created for Old Spice. Considered one of the most popular viral campaigns in history, the original spots showed the main character, a muscular, shirtless "Old Spice Man," transition from being in a bathroom, to a sailboat, to riding a horse on the beach, in a nonchalant demeanor and without pausing his monologue.

Yet, the body is nothing short of an incredible machine, which serves multiple purposes when we are sweating: cooling the body when it gets too hot and moisture evaporates; contributing to healing wounds; clearing the skin; eliminating BPA and producing natural antibiotics; among other things. So, sweating is quite good for you. So is another very natural human activity with a similarly bad reputation: making mistakes. Yet, as with sweating, we avoid mistakes at all costs, refusing to understand and fully embrace their benefits. Good things come to those who sweat.

LEARN TO FAIL. FAIL TO LEARN. AND REPEAT.

Make no mistake (no pun intended), accepting fault and making mistakes is a crucial part of growing up. We all make mistakes. We are all failures, in some way. There is no other choice in most cultures, organizations, and families. Some things in life are meant to be discovered only through trial and error. Some mistakes are unavoidable. We all reach critical points in our lives where our wisdom or knowledge is tested. We don't follow instructions, we take the wrong turn, file the wrong paperwork, get the wrong job, miss an important deadline, say the wrong thing, say the right thing at the wrong time, and more. In the business world, those mistakes lead to frequent post-mortems and corrective action plans. Of course, we attempt to keep failures to a minimum, because we are conditioned to think about mistakes as being bad. We get emotionally attached to the desirable outcome. Penalizing mistakes is an old cultural belief and stereotypical notion. Repeating mistakes over time can lead to drastic failure. That's failing backwards.

However, failure and setbacks are life companions we should not fear. We must take ownership of our failures. Failure can be the beginning of something special. Failure disciplines our basic expectations and encourages us to be open-minded and flexible. Failures favor risk-takers, as some mistakes are good and worth experiencing. The reality is that mistakes are nothing more than lessons to be learned. Embracing occasional failure frees us up to try more often, be more adventurous, and take chances. It's the difference between sinking or swimming.

*"A man should never be
ashamed to own he has been in
the wrong, which is but saying
... that he is wiser today than
he was yesterday."*

ALEXANDER POPE
English writer & poet

LEARN HOW TO FALL FORWARD
Let's admit it. Failure has a bad reputation in our society. No one anxiously or proudly speaks out about their failures. Uncertainty, fear, and ambiguity are everyday enemies that contribute to our fallouts. Yet great leaders are those who openly leverage failure to achieve success. The path to success is nothing but a series of failures to overcome and turn into growth opportunities.

One of the most undeniable qualities of successful individuals is their ability to pick themselves up after falling, reflect on how they found themselves in this situation in the first place, and reapply themselves. Where others see overpowering roadblocks, they see themselves being tested. Do you know of any success stories that aren't anchored to an obstacle course of failed attempts, resets, disappointments, and adversity? I personally can't think of one.

If you stop trying, your latest failure becomes permanent. We must let go of self-doubt and be unafraid of making mistakes. I know what you are thinking: easier said than done. That's true. How do we best prepare ourselves to take advantage of these learning opportunities? We must gather what knowledge we can from our failures and leverage it in the future for continuous improvement. We must recover from it. All failures and setbacks are opportunities for personal growth and learning.

YOU MAY NOT REALIZE HOW CLOSE YOU ARE TO SUCCESS. DON'T GIVE UP TOO EARLY.

This is a concept that innovative and fast-growing companies like Amazon, which provides "Earth's biggest selection of books, electronics, apparel & more," understands well. The Seattle-based company is a compelling case study in embracing risk and failure as core elements of its cultural and business practices. Failure is expected. They admitted failing many times, privately but also publicly. They will continue to fail because this is a part of their DNA. Failure is a healthy indicator of a culture that values speed and autonomy of decision-making.

Embracing failure as a necessary stepping stone toward success profoundly changes our perspective and invites us to be bolder and more ambitious, without fear of the consequences. We learn to be accountable. What we learn from our past mistakes—if they are not disastrous with permanent, insurmountable consequences—makes us stronger and better prepared to tackle new challenges.

No one likes to fail. But it's okay to fail or fall short of achieving certain goals. It's okay to be wrong trying to do right. It's okay to make mistakes and miss the mark. I've missed the mark quite a few times myself, both at a personal and professional level. I didn't realize then that these setbacks were essential to building character and preparing myself for even bigger challenges down the road. I was being tested. Without knowing it at the time, I was simply experimenting. In retrospect, the mistakes were small compared to the ones I faced later in life, but I was better prepared as a result.

Internationally acclaimed Australian actress and theatre director, Cate Blanchett, suggests a better way: go big and fail gloriously. Fail often, fail twenty times, pick yourself up twenty-one times. Rise again and again until you come through. The key to personal growth is experimentation. And to experiment, without knowing the real outcome of what you're going to do, you must fail.

TELL YOURSELF, "I WILL WHAT I WANT"
How can you stay on top during tumultuous times? It's hard to deal with failures, especially when you feel stuck or must recover quickly. The ability to pick oneself up, learn, break the mold, and go in a bold new direction requires that extra grit, daring, and spunk that only the wisest or strongest have. Not being afraid to fail shows tremendous confidence and authenticity, which encourages respect and collaboration. No one can be expected to make every mistake in the book and declare success. There are too many ways to fail, too many options to

choose from, and too little time to learn.

Of course, failing too much can surely demotivate and drain someone, no matter how committed they are to self-improvement. We may feel guilt, embarrassment, and even shame. The self-criticism process is emotionally unpleasant and, over time, can slowly but surely chip away at our self-esteem. We ask ourselves: Am I good enough? When we do, we face self-contempt—considering ourselves incapable of facing a challenge or viewing ourselves as undeserving—instead of accepting these failures as opportunities for growth.

Repeated failures can, and often do, lead to long term success. Every time we try something new and fall short of meeting our goal, it provides us valuable, actionable information about what went wrong and, obviously, what went right. Then we can make small changes, adjust our aim, and try again, continually learning and improving. It moves us forward, one mistake at a time. This is the message that footwear, sports, and casual apparel company, Under Armour, chose to emphasize in an inspiring 2014 campaign called "I will what I want," developed by their award-winning creative advertising agency Droga5.

> *"The greatest mistake you can make in life is to be continually fearing you will make one."*
>
> ———
>
> **ELBERT HUBBARD**
> *American writer, publisher, artist & philosopher*

The global brand campaign kicked off with a launch film featuring American ballerina Misty Copeland, and generated four million views in just one week. In the spot, Copeland receives a rejection letter, an example indicative of the constant negative feedback that the athlete had to overcome, telling her that she had the wrong body for ballet and at thirteen years old, she was simply too old to be considered. She failed forward beautifully, learning from these disappointments, eventually becoming a ballerina soloist at the American Ballet Theatre and the first African American female principal dancer at one of the three leading classical ballet companies in the United States. The television spot is moving. To me, Misty Copeland is a Success Freak.

You, too, must reject outcomes that do not align with your ambitions, and tell yourself that setbacks are simply part of the journey. Those who tell you that you can't do something are usually those who didn't try hard enough and failed. Only those who are determined can accept defeat and try persistently until they achieve success.

Look at motivational speaker and author Tony Robbins who overcame a very difficult childhood and is now such a powerful voice for those who share similar hardships and look up to him. We can easily relate to these tenacious icons, and that's why they inspire us. Every day, we fight for what we believe in. We cannot get hurt or defeated when we fight for what we love.

NOT ALL FAILURES ARE EQUAL: AVOID DOING TOO LITTLE TOO LATE

It wouldn't be fair to assume that we are all equal in our ability to learn from failures. It's not fair, perhaps, but it's true. Those who have a risk-averse mindset are constantly looking for ways to mitigate risk, because that gives them comfort and reassurance. A risk profile is one's ability to take on risks. The concept is particularly well known in the financial services industry as it determines how an investor's portfolio will be managed, whether conservatively or aggressively. If you are conservative, you might want to consider bonds and commodities which are likely to be less volatile than stock markets. If you are aggressive, you might be willing to consider high-growth companies like startup, tech, or biotech companies, which can deliver high returns, but may also fall short of meeting expectations.

What does this mean? Those individuals who accept failure as a learning mechanism are more likely to be aggressive in their approach and, therefore, take risks. They are more likely to learn faster than most people. A study by Michigan State University validated that people who think they can learn from mistakes exhibit a different brain reaction to those mistakes than those who don't. They are consciously aware of mistakes they make and can quickly adjust and bounce back from them. If you are conservative by nature, this may be an opportunity to let go of your fears and allow yourself to be vulnerable and acquire knowledge. Those who try again and again are ultimately getting better at what they do. They produce more—even if much of the quality is not yet good—but after many attempts, they produce higher quality work.

In his *TED Talk*, "The Surprising Habits of Original Thinkers," Adam Grant insists that "originals" feel fear like everyone else. He says, "They're afraid of failing, but what sets them apart from the rest of us is that they're even more afraid of failing to try. They know you can fail by starting a business that goes bankrupt or by failing to start a business at all. They know that in the long run, our biggest regrets are not our actions but our inactions. The things we wish we could redo, if you look at the science, are the chances not taken."

Aaron Kozbelt, a psychology professor at Brooklyn College and music aficionado, examined patterns of creativity over the lifespan of classical composers. He plotted how much some composers produced by an index of quality. The key takeaway: those who produced more compositions—like Beethoven, Mozart, and Bach—had a much higher chance of creating brilliant work. By improving their craft, through trial and error—accepting that they produced mediocre output at times—they eventually produced magnificent work and masterpieces that would transcend time and generations. They were risk takers who failed more often than they succeeded. If you want to be brilliant at what you do, do not do too little too late. Let go of your fears or the feelings that hold you back. There is always a light at the end of every tunnel. Leave your hesitations and flashlight behind, for they will slow you down. Life can be summed up by the risks taken.

 **TAKE ONLY CALCULATED RISKS OR BE PREPARED TO WEAR A HELMET FOR LIFE**
Canadian filmmaker James Cameron once explained that failure is an integral part of any process. In his opinion, any important endeavor require innovation and therefore, some risk. The former truck driver-turned-director, producer, and screenwriter responsible for major box-office successes like *The Terminator* (1984) and *Titanic* (1997) knows what he's talking about. His science-fiction epic *Avatar* (2009) was ten years in the making before its initial release, because Cameron had been waiting for the necessary technology to be advanced enough to create his project. To see his vision through, Cameron took the calculated risk to delay the launch, allowing for theatres worldwide to install 3D projectors. The risky move paid off, as the movie, almost entirely produced with computer-generated animation, became the highest grossing film of all time in the United States and Canada ($2.78 billion), breaking several box office records.

Of course, not all failures are created equal. Be selective about the risks you take on. What risks are you willing to take to propel your life forward? There are many types of risks: the silly ones that offer little insight or learning, and the calculated type that have been thought through carefully and could pay off. Some situations do not allow for risks to be evaluated. But often, one can evaluate different scenarios and decisions, and assess the level of risk compared to the potential upside before taking a leap. Do your homework and research potential out-comes before deciding. If the upside is not proportional to the risk, why bother?

When you take a calculated risk and fall short of seeing the desired outcome, it becomes a numbers game. The number one predictor of success becomes repetition. Most successes don't happen on a first try, or second, even third. We all remember that Thomas Edison invented the first commercially viable light bulb as well as the phonograph. Success Freaks must be experi-menters, willing to learn and test like Thomas Edison. Few of us know, however, that outside of these two famous inventions and patents, he also held 1,091 US patents in his name as well as many others in Europe—ranging from storage batteries to waterproofing fibers and fabrics. Edison's success as a prolific inventor came from a very small number of his discoveries. For Edison, failing was an essential part of the discovery process which he understood and embraced.

How often are you willing to take a calculated risk until you get to the right outcome? Most people wouldn't consider doing something a thousand times before giving up. Much has to do with your individual tolerance for pain. Emotional pain comes in different flavors: social rejection, embarrassment. Yet over-coming these symptoms is sometimes what it takes. Is it stub-bornness and absolute determination, boldness and courage? Or is it simple curiosity? In defiance, Thomas Edison said "I have not failed. I've just found 10,000 ways that won't work." How do you take calculated risks? Assess your options, evaluate the potential consequences, ask questions and make a choice as to how you want to proceed.

GO MUCH FASTER BY FALLING SMARTER

Speed skater Hiroyasu Shimizu of Japan can travel 500 meters in just 35.39 seconds, an average speed of 14.13 meters per second or 31.6 miles per hour. If you've ever had the opportunity to ice skate, you know that's pretty fast!

THE ART OF FALLING WELL

- ☐ ASSESS THE ENVIRONMENT CONSTANTLY
- ☐ EVALUATE AND ACCEPT RISKS
- ☐ LEARN TO FALL THE RIGHT WAY
- ☐ TRAIN AND IMPROVE OVER TIME
- ☐ MINIMIZE IMPACT AND AVOID INJURIES
- ☐ BOUNCE BACK AND RECOVER QUICKLY
- ☐ GAIN SPEED AND CONFIDENCE

Would you be surprised if I tell you that one of the most important ice-skating skills is falling? That's right, falling. Professional and competitive skaters fall frequently. For them, falling is just another important skill to develop so they can do it as safely as possible and avoid severe injuries. Learning to fall is also a skill that saves lives. An estimated 420,000 people per year die of bad falls worldwide, from slipping in the shower to tripping down the stairs. A lot more are injured and end up in the hospital.

By learning to fall the right way— knowing how to absorb the impact and avoiding severe injury—we recover quickly. These principles, which we apply to our physical environment, are no different from the emotional situations we encounter at work or at home. We must learn to prepare ourselves for the inevitable failures of testing, experimenting, exploring, and investigating the world and relationships around us. When we are prepared for it, the shock is lessened, and the impact reduced.

REMEMBER THAT ONCE IS A MISTAKE, BUT TWICE IS A CHOICE

I heard someone once say: "I never make the same mistake twice. I make it five or six times, just to be sure!" How about twenty or 100 times? How much time, blood or tears do you have stocked up to offer the world? Are you sabotaging yourself by repeating the same mistakes? How many times can you afford to fail? Learning always comes at a price; be willing to pay it. The behaviors that contribute to failed starts and wrecked relationships, that take people down a path of continued disappointment, can be avoided. Because we see mistakes as a symptom of our limited intellectual or emotional abilities, we feel sorry for ourselves and we fail to focus on what to do about it the next time around.

Clearly, embracing failures doesn't mean looking to

consistently fail. That would defeat its purpose. With every failure comes a lesson that must be learned and applied to future situations. Some refer to it as a learning culture. Simply stated, it means identifying errors and committing to not making the same mistake ever again. Frankly, who can afford to do so? The good news is that some failures are simply preventable. Any failed attempt

PREPARE YOURSELF FOR THE INEVITABLE FAILURES OF LIFE.

should be immediately followed by a sort of diagnostic and problem-solving process to isolate what can be learned and what is circumstantial.

In the professional world, it's commonly known as a postmortem. This is where people come together to share their observations, agree on improvement areas, and institute change to reflect on what was learned. Whether this is in a personal or professional situation, it's always advisable to formally document these conclusions so they aren't misunderstood or forgotten. While it's preferable to distance oneself from mistakes, we must do so without forgetting them, so we can refer to them when needed. Failure and actionable learning are inseparable twins.

 **LOOK INWARD TO AVOID THE BLAME GAME**
Accountability and ownership of failure is the signature of a leader—if you are brave enough to look inward to understand its origin and prompt course correction. We cannot learn

without taking full accountability for our mistakes and the role we played in contributing to them—or the role we didn't play, but should have. People are naturally inclined to downplay responsibility, dodge the bullets and place undue blame on external or situational factors. We blame our bosses, spouses, or neighbors for situations that we created or simply fueled by our inactions. Yet facing the truth can be particularly difficult. We get in full denial mode, dodge the bullets, and start the stress-releasing, but unhealthy process, of finger-pointing.

DO NOT FAIL BY DEFAULT, BY LIVING TOO CAUTIOUSLY.

Yes, we can all be hypocrites at times, and it takes remarkable courage to look at ourselves and face up to responsibilities. This psychological trick is known as "fundamental attribution error." It is defined as the tendency to explain someone's behavior based on internal factors, such as personality or disposition, and to underestimate the influence that external factors, such as situational influences, have on another person's behavior. How often do we play the blame game? Many of us do this daily. We blame others for our job situations, our relationship problems, our education (or lack of thereof). It's so much easier to point fingers at someone else than it is to look deep inside at our own behavior, fears, and attitudes, and how these contribute to our life decisions. Even if others are purposely getting in our way, we can follow the advice of American newscaster for NBC and ABC, David Brinkley. For Brinkley, to be successful at anything, you must be able to deal with critics and climb on the pile of bricks others may have thrown at you. I find this metaphor inspiring.

Life is a succession of false starts that may test our resolve and chip away at our confidence. These may even challenge our long-term vision. But we are our own weakest link and often quit too soon. I made that mistake once or twice in my life. I once launched a fashion company that was to disrupt the traditional men's suit business and made a few mistakes along the way: I underestimated the importance of building a sound and customer-centric backend. I misjudged the financial commitment required to launch a venture in this category. However, failing to make failure a growth opportunity is counter-productive over time. To become a Success Freak, you must grow mentally strong and choose to take corrective action. Get in front of the issue. If you don't deal with issues, they will deal with you.

STRENGTHENING THROUGH SETBACKS

 MISTAKES

WRONG **MISGUIDED**

INCORRECT
MISTAKEN
IMPRECISE

UNWISE
MISINFORMED
CONFUSED

= ACCEPTING
YOUR FAILURE

= LEARNING
FROM FAILURE

SUCCESS FREAK ACTIONS TO TAKE

 HAVE A POSITIVE ATTITUDE

 APPLY CONCLUSIONS

 TAKE CALCULATED RISKS

 TAKE ACCOUNTABILITY

FACE IT: WINNING IS ABOUT BOUNCING BACK

Although we may not always know how, we are all naturally inclined to bounce back when facing setbacks. We cannot change the strength or direction of the wind, but we can leverage it to propel our life forward. The formula for strengthening through setbacks requires us to maintain a positive attitude as we accept our mistakes and learn from them. We must then apply what we learn, evaluate the risks involved, and take accountability for our decisions and the role we played in the outcome. Obstacles test us; they test our patience and resolve. But don't sweat it, obstacles cannot stop a dream already in motion.

We are the hero of our own story when we give without asking, when we listen without judging, and when we lead without doubting. To be a Success Freak is to change our outlook and help us turn every failure into a stepping stone. Expect many on your journey. Don't hesitate to share your failures and struggles with others. It doesn't matter if it's work-related, if it's about failed relationships, broken dreams, or economic challenges. You will inspire others, build bridges, and connect with others.

Successful failures can be a way of life, not just a new mindset. We may be pushed to the ground, hurting and full of doubt. But when our time comes, we will pick ourselves up and bounce back. We will strengthen through setbacks and accomplish wonders—with a few elegant scars along the way to prove it.

EXERCISE #3

CONSIDER THIS EXERCISE TO COMPLETE THIS CHAPTER.
WRITE DOWN ANSWERS TO THE
FOLLOWING QUESTIONS:

1. What is the biggest mistake you've made in your life and how did it affect your behavior?

_____

_____

_____

_____

_____

_____

2. What do you fear most when making mistakes?

_____

_____

_____

_____

3. How have you overcome the pain of defeat in the past?

_____

_____

_____

_____

4. Have you ever made the same mistake twice? If so, what kept you from learning and applying yourself differently?

5. Do you feel that your current setbacks are due to elements outside of your control? If so, how do you plan to (re)gain accountability for future outcomes?

ACTION PLAN

Now that you have completed the exercise section and have reflected on ways you can build this new skill, it's time to act. Here are seven specific actions you must take to immediately apply what you've learned in this chapter:

CHALLENGE THREE:
LEARN TO FAIL SMART AND STRENGTHEN YOUR CHARACTER

- ☐ Fail forward. Consider every failed attempt moving forward as an opportunity for personal growth and improvement.

- ☐ Practice makes perfect. Tell yourself "I Will What I Want" and don't give up too early. Keep trying until you make it or learn from it.

- ☐ Do not waste time pointing fingers at others. Own it. Take full responsibility for your mistakes.

- ☐ Tell yourself, "Been there, done that." Apply what you've learned immediately. Never repeat the same mistakes twice.

- ☐ Don't be short-sighted or reckless. Evaluate all your options before making a move. Make sure the end justifies the means.

- ☐ Look for new learning opportunities. Make risk-taking an integral part of how you manage your life in the future. Push yourself.

- ☐ Embrace vulnerability and practice humility. Share the findings of your mistakes with people close to you, and learn from theirs, too.

DAY FOUR, SKILL FOUR

"I never dreamed
about success.
I worked for it."

———

ESTÉE LAUDER
American Businesswoman & Entrepreneur

4

MOVERS AND SHAKERS

DAY FOUR, SKILL FOUR

Be obsessively outcome-oriented

ESTIMATED READING TIME: TWENTY-ONE MINUTES

ESTIMATED EXERCISE TIME: FIFTEEN MINUTES

 The iconic tagline for shoe giant Nike, Inc., "Just do it," has become more than an empowering trademark since 1988. Even to this day, the slogan is easily recognized as one of the most famous, powerfully simple, yet inspiring, calls to action for those who believe anything is within their reach. That message, developed by Nike's creative advertising agency—independent Portland-based Wieden+Kennedy—has since appeared on t-shirts, baseball caps, tattoos, etc. as a symbol of determination and empowerment. The symbol helped increase Nike's share of the US sport-shoe market from eighteen percent to forty-three percent in 1998.

The increase is a remarkable accomplishment for any company in only ten years, let alone an Oregon-based firm founded in 1964 (then Blue Ribbon Sports) which raised a modest $1,000 in capital by its two partners, Bill Bowerman and Phil Knight whose goal was to distribute low-cost, high-quality Japanese athletic shoes to American consumers. In the early 60s, they managed to raise $8,000 in sales by selling shoes at local tracks. In 2016, leveraging its prevailing brand named after the Greek goddess of victory, the world's largest supplier of athletic shoes and apparel reported over $32 billion in revenue with the "Just do it" tagline becoming synonymous with the multinational brand. Nearly thirty years after its conception, the iconic tagline has been featured in hilarious clips of actor Shia LaBeouf screaming, "Just do it!" furiously at the camera for two minutes in a motivational rant that took the internet by storm.

ENABLE YOUR FUTURE TODAY BY TAKING IMMEDIATE ACTION. IT'S NEVER TOO EARLY TO ACT.

Why is that? Why does a simple statement have such profound impact in our society? Perhaps because most people never start the thing they insist they want or need to do, or if they do, often quit before seeing it through. The tagline "Just do it" is a bold, universal invitation to listen to our most natural instincts: acting while letting go of our hesitations or fears. It resonates with everyone. We wear it with pride: Stop wishing, start doing and make it happen.

SET IT IN MOTION OR GET OUT OF THE WAY

There are many heroes throughout history that have been defined by their ability and willingness to act and see their visions come to life. These go-getters were obsessively outcome-oriented. They changed the world by turning ideas, vision, and inspiration into unequivocal, tangible results. No idea is real until it is brought to life. Nothing is brought to life until it is set in motion.

The world has always smiled upon movers and shakers throughout history. In December 1942, British Prime Minister, Winston Churchill exemplified the need for action when he issued a warning to landing craft designers, tasked with transporting tanks and troops across the Channel, to focus on the outcome instead of design considerations. Churchill used these words which still resonate today: "'The maxim 'Nothing avails but perfection' may be spelt shorter: 'Paralysis.'"

More recently, look at Greek-Italian-American businessman and philanthropist, John Paul DeJoria, known for the Paul Mitchell line of hair products and the Patrón Spirits Company. DeJoria, who grew up in a foster home and was a former street gang member, held jobs ranging from a janitor to insurance salesman before starting John Paul Mitchell Systems, with hairdresser Paul Mitchell, with a $700 loan. Even though his high school math teacher told him that he would never succeed at anything in life, and he had been fired from more than one job for not fitting in, while exceeding sales targets, DeJoria had a clear vision for what he wanted to accomplish and the desire to turn his bold ideas into something concrete and tangible: high performance products that solved customer problems. He took control of his life, and through his actions realized the outcomes he desired. There is no doubt that DeJoria is a Success Freak. Reflecting on these inspiring examples of obsessively outcome-oriented individuals, you might ask yourself: How does one overcome the illusion of perfection, the danger of paralysis, and the tough circumstances of life to become such a notable mover and shaker? Why can't you just do it, too?

YESTERDAY YOU SAID, "TOMORROW"

That's right. Yesterday you said, "tomorrow!" There is a reason for that. Let me ask you: Are you feeling overwhelmed at times? Do you get easily distracted during the day? Are you growing frustrated by your inability to get everything done at work and at home? Do you want to boost your productivity but don't know how? Do you feel stuck at times? Do you find it difficult to say "no?" If this all sounds familiar, you might fall into the devastating procrastination trap that swallows millions every day.

Procrastination is the greatest enemy to being successful, no matter your definition. When we fail to act, we give up on the ability to learn and move our agenda forward. Let's be realistic. It's so easy at times to delay decisions, postpone taking important action, put off making difficult decisions, and push out important milestones until the very last moment. Taking action to get things moving at home or at work can be stressful at times. Can you think of a few things you should already be doing? Do you have a "to do" list somewhere getting dusty by the minute? Do you wait until the last minute to get something done? Are you growing tired of procrastinating, losing focus, and leaving projects often unfinished? Don't be alarmed. We all do this.

We procrastinate so much all day long, we are often

exhausted by dusk, but it's not without consequences. Consider the stress you experience by putting things off too long. We get so busy doing things we don't need to do to avoid the things we are supposed to be doing. To use the colloquial expression: Isn't it time to "shit or get off the pot"?

DARE TO MAKE THE IMPOSSIBLE POSSIBLE.

This is nothing more than a vulgar rephrasing of the old New England expression "Fish or cut bait." But you get the idea. There is no room for procrastination among Success Freaks.

~~SHOULD; WOULD; COULD~~ DID

In 1974, a young professor of architecture in the charming city of Budapest, Hungary, created a working prototype of a multidimensional object that defied plausibility—a solid cube that could twist and turn. This unusual object would become the world's best-selling toy ever, played with by an estimated one in seven people alive and more than 350 million products sold since launching in 1980. This object was a cube with colorful stickers on its sides that could be rotated to scramble the colors, with the objective of matching them up again.

We know it as the "Rubik's Cube" or "Magic Cube," and part of its allure was that there were 43,252,003,274,489,856,000 (43 quintillion) ways that one could complete the puzzle. To put this into perspective, if you were to turn a Rubik's Cube once every second, it would take you 1.4 TRILLION YEARS to go through all the permutations, enough to give anyone a big headache just contemplating this fact. Yet, the best "speed-cubers" (the names given to competitors trying to solve the cube as quickly as possible) can solve the cube in under six seconds.

The now-famous professor, inventor and architect who came up with the brilliant concept was named Ernő Rubik, another Success Freak. He invented many mechanical puzzles. Originally, the Rubik's Cube was meant to be an object of art, a sort of mechanical sculpture for its inventor who liked to highlight the profound contrasts in the human condition: simplicity and complexity, order and chaos, stability and motion. The cube was meant to be a way to teach architectural students about three-dimensional space. Soon enough, the object became a worldwide phenomenon, driven by the ingenuity and tenacity of a Hungarian mover and shaker, committed to making a difference by turning his ideas into major success. Ernő Rubik believed that curious individuals find puzzles in every aspect of life which can be solved with enough determination.

Looking at a problem is never good enough. Like the Rubik's Cube, you often know exactly what you need to do, but get frustrated when the answer doesn't come easily. Only those who solve problems—who take them head-on and see them through—will experience the sweet satisfaction that can only result from taking action.

We take comfort in believing we can do anything in life, but the real satisfaction comes from getting it done. Published in the 1990s, the popular book *The Power of Now: A Guide to Spiritual Enlightenment* by Eckhart Tolle guides readers through steps on how to live in the present moment and avoid being paralyzed by the past or the future. There have been many books on this topic, many of which are drawing insight from psychology, meditation, Eastern wisdom like Buddhism, and Western culture about getting "stuff done."

Psychology tells us that the concept of "delayed action" is an adult trait, often associated with maturity. For example, a child is more likely to act spontaneously, going right from impulse to action: I want this toy, so I will just grab it. As we mature and grow up, we learn to slow down our impulses, adding an important step between impulse and action: thinking. We often refer to these decisions as "delayed gratifications" or "impulse control." There are many other factors that get in the way: fear, anxiety, conflicts, discouragement, self-doubt and indecision. However, when we learn to unleash the undeniable power of NOW, we start living in the moment, resisting negative, paralyzing forces and embracing outcomes.

I spent nearly a decade at Microsoft, headquartered in Redmond, Washington. Software companies are known to be fast-moving business environments where decisive actions make a difference between corporate success or failure, or between a short or long career. Among the many company values, one of them was a significant contributor to a culture of action. Employees were expected to be "accountable for commitments, results and quality to customers, shareholders, partners, and employees." Netflix's company values invite employees of the American entertainment company to "focus on results over process." Amazon has a "bias for action" in its leadership principles: "Speed matters in business. Many decisions and actions are reversible and do not need extensive study. We value calculated risk taking."

I recall participating in a very popular training session at that time, inspired by productivity consultant and coach, David Allen, who authored *Getting Things Done: The Art of Stress-Free Productivity*. The key principles and productivity concepts (do it, delegate it, defer it, drop it) were particularly useful to manage an inbox that reached astronomical levels every day, keeping up with the pace without wearing down. Working for a global company like Microsoft meant that I was having calls with Europe in the morning, meetings with my colleagues in the US, and more calls with Asia in the

BALANCE RISKS AND REWARDS WHEN YOU ACT. BUT INACTION HAS FAR GREATER RISKS.

evening. Keeping up with hundreds of emails was important, but getting tasks done, prioritizing, and delivering results were the ultimate test. One day, I was privileged to receive the Marketing Excellence award on stage from then-Microsoft CEO Steve Ballmer himself. Ballmer, the energetic executive and current owner of the Los Angeles Clippers NBA team, replaced Bill Gates as CEO in 2000. This prestigious award was a defining career accomplishment for me but also had a personal meaning. Hard work and being obsessively outcome-oriented paid off.

Here is the take-away: we must perform immediate actions or be unconditionally overwhelmed, one procrastinated decision at a time. "Might." "Could." "Would." There is no room for those words in your new, Success Freak vocabulary.

DON'T CONFUSE MOTION WITH PROGRESS

We often confuse motion with progress, activity with productivity. Activity does not always translate into productivity. Are you effectively getting things done, taking a jump or are you just dipping your toes in the water or running around like a chicken with its head cut off? Taking action doesn't imply keeping busy or nervously jumping from one activity to another. If you want to research a few websites to complete a report, or tell a few colleagues of yours that you are working on it, one might consider this being in "motion" or an "activity." But if you write and send that report, you can call this "progress" or "productivity."

On May 9, 2015, Oscar-award-winning actor Denzel Washington spoke at the Dillard University commencement ceremony and shared words of wisdom: he reminded the young audience that because people are doing a lot more means that they are getting a lot more done. Washington insisted that most people confuse movement with progress. His mother, Lennis Washington, once told him that he could run and play all the time and never get anywhere. Washington's mother asserted that real progress comes from the constant commitment to strive, to have goals and to move forward.

Sustained progress is the ability to say "no" to old distractions and "yes" to new opportunities. Don't let yourself be fooled by how busy you are and how packed your calendar is. You might be fooling others for a while, but reality will catch up with you quickly.

If you use time wisely, you might even accomplish more by doing less. Leading organizations do not reward employees that demonstrate they are constantly in motion, talking about what they might do, could do, would do, without acting or moving any closer to their end goal. Market leaders reward employee and team performance, impact and measurable results. They reward movers and shakers that propel them forward. The outcomes resulting from these efforts is the ultimate measure of accomplishment and advancement.

BALANCE PASSIVE THINKING WITH ACTIVE DOING

Don't just think about it or say it, do it. Knowledge and dialog without acting is wasteful. Jumping into action without thinking or communicating is careless and dangerous. Too much thinking or talking can also create inertia. Too little can create unrecoverable disasters. What's the right balance? Should we listen to our hearts more than our brains? Should we talk less and do more? Do we perform better when we don't overthink?

A study by researchers Timothy Wilson and Jonathan Schooler supports that experts, when performing at their best, don't think about what they are doing as they are doing it, acting intuitively. In the *Journal of Personality and Social Psychology* where they published their results, they concluded that, "at times, the unexamined choice is worth making." This is consistent with the conclusions reached by Malcom Gladwell in this best-seller book, *Blink*, where the author presents many compelling examples of expert choices and impactful actions made in the blink of an eye, without thinking.

> "Without knowledge action is useless and knowledge without action is futile."
>
> ———
>
> **ABU BAKR**
> *Companion and father-in-law of the Islamic prophet Muhammad*

In everyday life, however, successful individuals are the ones effective at balancing strategy and execution. We must think like an individual of immediate action, and act like an individual of deliberate thought. Being obsessively outcome-oriented does not mean jumping at every opportunity to take action. No one is recommending that people should act based on hasty judgment or a gut reaction, without some consideration—or what some refer to as "failing to plan is planning to fail."

Conversely, emphasizing thinking over action leads to second-guessing oneself, inertia, and lost opportunities. This is what is also known as "analysis paralysis," when you overthink or over-analyze a situation so that a decision or action is never taken. We all want to make good decisions. But even the right decisions alone have no impact without making something happen. The best ideas or strategies are worthless if they can't be implemented.

Speaker and consultant Ellory Wells firmly believes that we have an unlimited supply of ideas and that the real value lies in getting things done. For Wells, the most challenging obstacle is getting started. Don't get in your own way. Russian-born American computer scientist and internet entrepreneur Sergey Mikhaylovich Brin believes that exceptional execution and delivery are far more important than coming up with good ideas. Brin would know. Together with Larry Page, these two Success Freaks co-founded Google in 1998 while they were PhD students at Stanford University. We can agree that Brin's actions, as well as his ideas, profoundly changed the way we access information.

When strong ideas fuel prevailing actions, they become unstoppable; balance is key. If you do too much talking, how much time do you have left to do things? If you do too much thinking, it's probably because you are not breaking big problems and challenges into more manageable, actionable solutions. In other words, the less we act, the less likely we are to improve our ability to think and therefore make better decisions. The secret is in the careful equilibrium of the two. If you can master this, you may have something worth talking about later on.

SET THE RIGHT PRIORITIES TO GET MORE STUFF DONE

If you write a to-do list of everything that comes to mind, you may realize that it looks like a never ending amount of work and effort. The list may end up being paralyzing, accomplishing the exact opposite of what you would hope. If something takes less than five-to-ten minutes, don't bother writing it down, especially if it takes you about the same amount of time to capture it in your Smartphone or a notebook. Your to-do list should only include activities and projects that will require a sizeable amount of time, energy or resources to accomplish. That's the first tip on how to prioritize.

There will never be enough time in a day to get everything done and you can't please everyone. Unlikely to change, this is probably why time management is one of the most popular book topics of all time, with hundreds of titles promising to change your life. We are easy targets: time is in limited supply and as such, we are all looking for tricks, tips, and solutions to get more done in less time. The only alternative to getting things done faster and more productively is to learn to focus on the most important tasks and make sure they get completed successfully. Sometimes it also means saying "no" or "not now" to those around us to avoid veering off track.

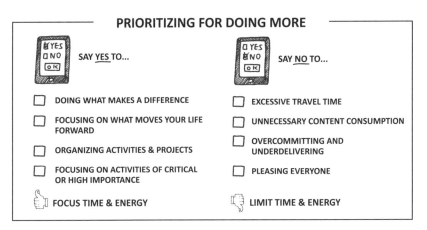

It's liberating to respectfully decline tasks or activities that previously consumed so much time and energy without moving us forward. Saying "no" to others often means saying "yes" to you and your unlimited potential. Are you curbing your social media addiction? Are you effectively handling the productivity-killing effect of media consumption like television, gaming, mobile, and internet browsing by limiting your intake and balancing your time wisely? Are you avoiding time-wasting activities in your everyday life that keep you from focusing on the things that matter most?

Here are a few ways to combat these time-sucking habits: Reduce content consumption that does not provide much educational value. Reduce travel time that is unnecessary. Use technology—phone, email, computers—whenever possible to streamline paperwork, automate repetitive tasks, and simplify many aspects of your life. Some refer to it as "eating that frog," a metaphor for prioritizing and tackling the most challenging tasks. Setting priorities encourages us to get the right things done first, so we can focus all our time and energy on what makes a difference.

Tell yourself that you only have time to accomplish a few tasks each day. It might require labeling each item on your to-do list based on its relative importance, using a four-point scale for example (critical, high, medium, low). There is no magic silver bullet, and it might seem a bit subjective. Don't over-commit yourself. Make sure you have the time and resources needed. Focus on what matters most. No one, however, is better equipped than you are to determine what is of upmost importance and what is not. So, make a list, rank it and prioritize what needs to be done.

> "The superior man is modest
> in his speech, but exceeds in
> his actions."
>
> ---
>
> ## CONFUCIUS
> *Chinese teacher, editor, politician,
> and philosopher*

AVOID THE TRAP OF PERFECTIONISM
How frequently do you hold back on sharing your work until it is perfect? Are you the type of individual who doesn't want to provide less than top-notch quality work? Success Freaks tend to be perfectionists. They aim high and are demanding of others and themselves. They relentlessly pursue their objectives and seek to reach the unattainable: perfection.

Anything short of achieving the perfect outcome might be considered undesirable and therefore unworthy of action. Do you ever wait for the perfect conditions before you do something? Would you rather postpone doing something than risk the chance that it may fall short? If you're guilty of these evasions, you know exactly what I am talking about. This is something I still personally struggle with, but am getting better at. We must focus on getting things done, moving us forward rather than chasing perfection.

In the process, don't confuse abilities with accomplishments, or skills with outcomes. What matters is what you actually do with your life. To accomplish our goals, we must accept whatever circumstances are thrown at us, we must face whatever roadblocks get in the way, and still move forward with determination. We also need to get our hands dirty and focus on the small details in life to walk the talk. We often hear people around us suggest we focus on "the big picture" and not sweat the small stuff. Yep, maybe, but this is not how you get things done.

"Perfect is the enemy of good," said French philosopher and prolific writer, Voltaire. How do we make things happen, with less effort and stress? How do we release more creativity, energy, and outcomes in what we do? Attention to detail matters. In the end, we must capitalize on our strengths. Put yourself out there, even if you are not one hundred percent ready. Test the waters and embrace your natural bias toward action and "put some water in your wine" as the French say. Don't wait for the perfect plan or circumstances. Those don't exist. Get things going, adjust as you go.

DEVELOP YOUR PERSONAL ("GETTING SHIT DONE") STYLE
Don't wait patiently for opportunities to show up at your doorstep. Get out there and knock on every door you see. Do you have your prioritized to-do list ready to go? Are you pumped up and ready to get down to business?

It's time for action and you are ready to move mountains. You will face many challenges along the way, no doubt. Not everyone may agree with our decisions and actions—well, too bad for them. In life, we inevitably encounter people whose job or natural bias is to say "Are you sure you want to do this?" As the expression goes: it's easier to ask for forgiveness than permission. So, don't ask. Don't wait for someone to give you the green light; seize the moment and make your move. We find ample reasons to slow down, stop, or delay decisions. However, to become successful, we will need to embrace the incredible power of action and let go of bad habits that have been holding us back for too long.

Have clarity of purpose. Turn your ideas and energy into prioritized outcomes and measurable results. Stay the course no matter what.

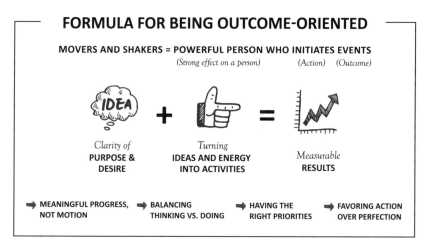

How do you make the impossible possible? Stop trying, start doing. In life, you will meet thinkers, talkers, and doers. You need to be all three, but ideally, in the right sequence: think, do, and

EXERCISE #4

CONSIDER THIS EXERCISE TO COMPLETE THIS CHAPTER.
WRITE DOWN ANSWERS TO THE
FOLLOWING QUESTIONS:

1.   How do you currently organize all your tasks and to-do lists
so you can easily access and review them?

_____

_____

_____

_____

_____

2.   Do you feel that your current approach to managing all your
deliverables is effective enough? If not, what could you do differently?

_____

_____

_____

_____

_____

3. How do you stay focused and prioritize your activities today to make
the most effective use of your time and efforts?

_____

_____

_____

_____

_____

_____

4. Are you prepared to confidently say "no" or delegate to make your life far more productive than it is today?

_____

_____

_____

_____

_____

5. How do you track your progress against your goals and what decisions do you make if you fall behind?

_____

_____

_____

_____

_____

DAY FOUR, SKILL FOUR
ACTION PLAN

Now that you have completed the exercise section and have reflected on ways you can build this new skill, it's time to act.
Here are seven specific actions you must take to immediately apply what you've learned in this chapter:

CHALLENGE FOUR:
BE OBSESSIVELY OUTCOME-ORIENTED

☐ Minimize daily distractions by reducing screen time, for example, and avoid wasteful activities (let's be honest: you know what they are)! Free up time to do things that matter.

☐ Set clear priorities and measurable goals so you can laser-focus on the most important tasks and activities to propel you forward.

☐ Make productive use of your life by working diligently through your to-do list. Infuse your life with action.

☐ Do not postpone important tasks that can be done today. Live with a constant sense of urgency. Say no again and again to demands that don't move you forward.

☐ Don't overthink to the point of inaction, but act with enough knowledge so you are most effective at what you do.

☐ When it's time to act, trust your instincts. Favor actionable ideas and tangible results over perfection.

☐ Remind yourself that success is never a popularity contest: it's better to be disliked for what we do than loved for what we don't do.

DAY FIVE, SKILL FIVE

"It's not about having enough time, it's about making enough time."

RACHAEL BERMINGHAM
Australian Entrepreneur, Author & Public Speaker

5

IT'S FIVE O'CLOCK
SOMEWHERE

DAY FIVE, SKILL FIVE

Accomplish more by mastering the effective use of time

ESTIMATED READING TIME: TWENTY-FOUR MINUTES

ESTIMATED EXERCISE TIME: FIFTEEN MINUTES

 Has anyone jokingly told you, "It's five p.m. somewhere," to justify having a drink, or when inviting you to share one at an odd hour of the day? Five p.m. being the end of the work day for the traditional "nine-to-five" worker, it's an opportune time to go to the pub or local bar for some down time. The popular expression was later immortalized by a hit song by the same name from artists Alan Jackson and Jimmy Buffett:

> *Pour me somethin' tall an' strong.*
> *Make it a "Hurricane," before I go insane.*

It's only half past twelve. But I don't care,
it's five o'clock somewhere.

Well, if it's five p.m. somewhere in the world, technically speaking, it is also five a.m. somewhere else in the world. According to data from Edison Research, the peak time to wake up for most Americans is between six and 6:30 a.m. As a matter of fact, twenty-three percent rise during that time window. Seventeen percent wake up later than eight a.m.—slackers, you know who you are! However, only eight percent are awake by five a.m. It's so early that you are either waking up or going to sleep.

We know intuitively that those who wake up early seem to start the day with a slight advantage. My father used to quote me this French expression: "*l'avenir appartient à ceux qui se lèvent tôt.*" Translation: "The future belongs to those who wake up early." The expression is presumed to come from the nineteenth century before electricity was a tool for modern life. Those who woke up before the sun rose would have enough time to work a full day and, therefore, make a better living.

WAKE UP EARLY AND, IF THAT DOESN'T WORK, GO TO BED LATE

Go-getters who wake up before six a.m. want enough time to get what they need completed. I looked at what research I could find to correlate early rising with success. Various studies of CEOs and top executives concluded that eighty percent wake up at 5:30 a.m. or earlier. An article by *Business Insider* pointed to General Motors' CEO Dan Akerson and Apple's CEO Tim Cook, who rarely sleep past 4:30 a.m.; Virgin America's CEO David Cush, wakes up even earlier at 4:15 a.m.; and the list of high-profile CEOs rising early goes on.

Here is the catch: you can't master your life until you master your time. What if I told you that there are seven fundamental rules for managing time efficiently? Is waking up early one of them? Unfortunately, no one knows what they are. Seriously, if we did, books about time management would not occupy so many shelves in digital and physical bookstores, would they? But it won't stop us from highlighting time management techniques you can put to practice to master your own time.

I know how you feel, we are all so busy at work and at home. But are we truly productive? And perhaps equally important: How do we use our time efficiently and accomplish work/life balance? Timothy Ferriss, the brilliant author of *Live Anywhere, and Join the New Rich* and *Tools of Titans* interviewed more than 200 world-class performers ranging from celebrities, athletes, special operations commanders, and black-market biochemists. One of the questions he asked: "What does your morning routine look like?" The answers range from meditating, exercising, to eating healthy. So yes, the concept of effective time management goes far beyond when we start the day, or how many events occupy our day. It's about using that day most effectively. But would it hurt if you started your day earlier to get a head start? We know the answer to that question.

Let's be realistic, whether you're an early bird or late riser, the real question is: how do you make effective use of your time so every minute counts and add up to something meaningful? Regardless of whether you choose to wake up every morning by five a.m., make sure to fully enjoy your morning routine, or it will never stick. If you can't make it a habit, you will fall back on previous ways, trust me. I tried to stick to a routine that didn't sit too well with me or my wife (we will blame the loud alarm clock!). DNA studies show that some people are genetically inclined to be a morning or a night person.

According to my 23andMe 's DNA results, people with my genetics in their forties wake up on average around 7:48 a.m. on their days off, which proves to be relatively accurate for me. Check out your own wake up predictions based on your DNA and see if this is consistent with your current routine or bed time preferences. Keep in mind that, as you get older, people naturally wake up earlier.

No matter our predisposition, we have a lot of control over how we manage, and ultimately master, time. Let's take a closer look at some ageless principles and techniques to help you accomplish more by managing time better and smarter.

> *"A man who dares to waste one hour of time has not discovered the value of life."*
>
> ---
>
> **CHARLES DARWIN**
> *English naturalist, geologist and biologist*

DON'T GRAB THAT MARSHMALLOW YET
The eighteenth-century French naturalist and mathematician, Georges-Louis Leclerc has been quoted as saying, "Genius is nothing but a great aptitude for patience." Would you be willing and able to delay gratification if you thought it was worth the wait?

In the late 1960s, Walter Mischel, an American psychologist specializing in personality theory and social psychology, conducted studies with preschoolers, evaluating the self-control processes and mental mechanisms that enable an individual to forego immediate gratification to obtain a larger desired, but delayed, reward.

The experiment administered at the Bing Nursery School at Stanford, coined as the "Marshmallow Experiment," started with one of the research subjects facing a plate on which a marshmallow was placed. The child was told that if he/she didn't eat the marshmallow while the researcher stepped out, he/she would receive a second one. The choice couldn't be more obvious: eat one now or wait and enjoy two later. What would you do? The experiment showed some of the children— immediately or after a minute or two—seizing the opportunity to eat their one marshmallow, while others resisted the temptation long enough to get a second one. The experiment, first published in 1972, continued for years.

The follow-up studies with the test subjects involved tracking each child's progress across many aspects of their lives. Guess what happened? The longer an individual delayed gratification and the longer he or she could wait as a young child, the better he or she would do later in life at numerous measures. The test subjects willing to wait and delay gratification consistently showed better school results, including higher SAT scores, better social and cognitive functioning, better stress management skills, a lower level of substance abuse, and lower probability of being obese or going to jail.

The lesson from this experiment is obvious: if you are both willing and capable of waiting for something that is more promising than simply getting immediate gratification, you are more likely to make better choices over time. Being patient is a trait of individuals looking to making things happen, which is critical to succeeding in life. Maybe this is why authorities refer to the "10,000-hour rule," based on a study of violin students at a German music academy,

UNDERSTAND THE REAL VALUE OF TIME AND PRACTICE DELAYED GRATIFICATION IN MODERATION.

which suggests that anyone looking to become a top-notch professional, no matter the field or expertise area, requires intense, deliberate practice for a minimum of 10,000 hours. That would require practicing every minute you are awake for about a year and a half, or about three hours a day for nearly a decade, if you live a relatively normal life. That's the epitome of delayed gratification if you ask me.

There are many situations that present themselves where being patient is often necessary to gain more than would otherwise be possible. I tend to think about it like writing a book: it's a laborious, time-consuming project that has far greater reach than writing a blog, getting the word out there quickly.

The wait is worth it, when you consider the additional depth that can be achieved, and the greater reach and value obtained by an audience. Keep in mind, however, that the evil twin of self-control is procrastination, so practice delayed gratification in moderation.

AVOID DEADLY TIME TRAPS
LIKE THE PLAGUE

How much time are you spending on social media or watching television? We must decide if we are creators or mere consumers of content; there is not enough time to do both. Time traps are all around us. Can we spot them before these time wasters swallow us into the giant pit of randomization and irrelevancy? I sure hope so.

Everyone seems to have their favorite list of distractors, and you will find many in online blogs and articles—from spending countless hours on social media sites browsing mindless posts, watching silly videos, and playing mobile games, to meetings without clear agendas, and the traditional water cooler gossip conversations at work that go far beyond productive professional networking discussions. Pick your favorite. We waste time every day and are all guilty of it. Our attention span is increasingly short, especially with the abundance of technology and media vehicles all around us. We are human, and because of that, we must accept our innate desire for occasional distractions and fun activities that add up to nothing fruitful. So being unhuman is clearly not the solution. Like drinking, it requires some moderation.

Some of these time wasters are extremely addictive. Check out the list of most downloaded apps for the iPhone, Windows, or Android phones; it's not apps in the productivity section.

Games represent the most downloaded category by a large margin. Millions of users spend countless time slicing fruits as a Ninja, navigating perilous cliffs, impersonating an uphill racer, confronting zombies or fire wielding wizards, or using slingshots to fling birds at towers. Name your poison. It's all there, free or not, ready to consume the greatest asset you will ever own: time. To avoid time wasters and become a time master, one must set boundaries for a healthy, sustainable balance of activities that do not get in the way of accomplishing purposeful activities.

FOCUS YOUR TIME IN SHORT, TIMED INTERVALS

Director of Research at Harvard Business School, Teresa Amabile has published over 150 scholarly articles about psychology, innovation, and creativity inside organizations. Among her theories and findings, Amabile's research on driving productivity showed that achieving minor steps forward is highly motivating. Amabile claims that big wins are as important as they are. In her opinion, even small wins have a huge impact on boosting inner work life and motivating people. It's therefore important to realize "small wins" in short-timed intervals.

How do we avoid the distractions that are all around us and stay hyper focused? One technique worth considering is the Pomodoro Technique, invented in the late 1980s by entrepreneur Francesco Cirillo, and named after the tomato-shaped timer he used to track his tasks as a student ("*Pomodoro*" is the Italian word "tomato"). It's likely you might already be practicing this technique at times without realizing it. The simple yet effective concept, which is also known as timeboxing and used in software design, is as follows: Estimate what needs to be done and break all your work into short-timed intervals (typically twenty-five minutes in length) that are spaced out by short breaks of approximately five minutes. The intervals allow you to focus for short periods of time and stay on task until the timer rings. After each task, or a few tasks are completed, take a short break until you resume your tasks. The breaks simply give you a boost of energy and keep your creative juices pumping.

If you have an office job, you are likely to divide up your calendar in one-hour increments. Why? Well, because that's the way most software calendars work. You don't have time to fall into that trap, either. Schedule fifteen, thirty, or forty-five-minute meetings, and claim the remaining minutes in the hour for getting more accomplished. I made that change in my schedule and I suddenly did more with less time because, well, I had to. I used the remaining time to prepare for my next meetings or to get things done in between. It works.

DON'T FORGET TO RECHARGE YOUR BATTERIES

It's practically impossible to talk about the effective use of time without addressing the touchy topic of work/life balance. The concept of "balance" implies that we compartmentalize our time between our personal and professional activities. The reality is often quite different, especially when we do what we love for a living. It tends to be more about work/life choices and how they work together seamlessly, in complete harmony. If you are one of the lucky ones, your work is not that separate from your personal interests. Of course, you still have many personal or family responsibilities. When you are at the office or in a meeting, you can't stop being a loyal friend, a responsible parent, or a loving spouse. You can't get so busy that you fail to allow for these essential pieces of life to co-exist and overlap in a healthy way. In addition to taking care of others, you also need to dedicate enough time to take care of yourself.

To be at your best, you need to rest. Stanford business professor, Jeffrey Pfeffer, studied successful executives and analyzed the qualities they all had in common. The top quality wasn't the usual suspects—intelligence, talent, or interpersonal skills. The number one quality was energy levels. Most ambitious individuals don't value the benefits of rest and sleep in the way they should, until they learn that lesson the hard way. Be smart and give yourself plenty of rest and repair time. They say that the best way to recharge batteries is to unplug them. If you are still curious to know how long you can go without sleeping, be aware that Randy Gardner holds the scientifically documented record for the longest period of time a human has intentionally gone without sleep: 264 hours or eleven days.

Life is a marathon, not a sprint. If you have superpowers and can fly, do it; life often demands it. However, no one can effectively sustain it over extended periods of time. We all need time to think, step back and reflect. We also all need time for recovery. We can't function productively when we are perpetually stressed, overworked, and overcommitted. Dedicate enough time for sleep and exercise, and schedule time to maintain important relationships and hobbies in your life. When you do, you'll become far more engaged and alert, and your productivity will soar. This is also the opinion of Amazon founder, Jeff Bezos, who touts getting eight hours of sleep to be more productive, more excited, and more energized. According to Bezos, if you cut on sleep too much, you might feel that you are getting more productive for a while, but this productivity again is nothing more than an illusion. Bezos believes in quality over quantity, especially when you spend your time making decisions or interacting with people.

This is also validated by economic data. According to the ranking of the world's most productive employees, provided by the Organization for Economic Cooperation and Development (OECD), the US ranked only third in terms of GDP (gross domestic product) per hour worked, behind Norway and Luxembourg. This data gives an idea as to which countries make the most money in the least amount of time—and are therefore the most productive. Yet, when comparing that data to average annual hours actually clocked per worker, the US ranks thirteenth with 1,783 hours compared to Norway at 1,424 and Luxembourg at 1,512. So, we work more in the US, and generate less GDP than other countries like Luxembourg and Norway.

France, notoriously known for its generous annual leave (approximately thirty days per year of paid vacation, compared to fifteen days off in the US) reports 1,472 hours worked, ranking thirty-first on the list, but ranking sixth in terms of GPD—showing that working less and taking more holidays doesn't necessarily impact productivity. The lesson here is that dedicating enough time to recharge batteries is wise. So, catch your breath once in a while in between sprints, and you will keep going longer and faster.

> *"Those who make the worst
> use of their time are the first
> to complain of its brevity."*
>
> ———
>
> ## JEAN DE LA BRUYÈRE
> *French philosopher and moralist*

DO ONE THING AT A TIME, BUT DO IT WELL
If it's important to you, you will make time. We tend to multitask all day long, juggling between phone calls, emails, and texts while we are having conversations. We talk while we drive, check messages from the bathroom, and check social media feeds in meetings. However, more often than not, multitasking gets in the way of real performance and productivity. We overestimate our ability to do well while multitasking. It reduces our ability to filter, focus our attention, sustain our focus, listen well, recall information, and slows down our ability to make good decisions.

The brain can't multitask all that well—according to Adam Gazzaley (professor at the University of California San Francisco in the Departments of Neurology, Physiology, and

Psychiatry), along with California State University Dominguez Hills Professor Emeritus of psychology, Larry Rosen. In their book *The Distracted Mind: Ancient Brains in a High-Tech World*, they make the compelling case that our brains are limited in their ability to pay attention. The solution? Well, I don't believe it's a digital detox. We all rely increasingly on technology to get things done and it's not going away. To the contrary, technology, when used wisely, can be a powerful timesaver—but we don't always need it. Instead, we must engage in one task at a time, do each task as time-efficiently as possible, and if needed set aside technology-related distractions that do not increase productivity. You read that right. Yes, it's okay to set that phone down or turn that computer off for a while, then put all your mental energy into that single task to avoid mistakes and get the best possible outcome on your first try—instead of having to redo that task.

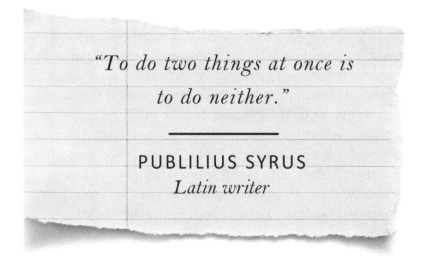

"*To do two things at once is to do neither.*"

PUBLILIUS SYRUS
Latin writer

CHANGE YOUR LIFE WITH THE 6D PRODUCTIVITY RULE
Don't fool yourself, success is hard work. It's not surprising that motivational speakers claiming otherwise might be popular. Who doesn't want a four-day work week or a four-hour work day? Especially if you consider what you do to be "work," and you are looking to minimize the amount of time and energy you need to dedicate to your daily activities.

Let's think about this differently. First, you must put in the time and give it your all to see outstanding results. Second, time alone is not enough to get you there; productive time is what we must embrace. Only when our time is spent wisely and productively do we realize the outcomes we seek. Set daily priorities, say "no" to time wasters or asks that do not move you forward, and dedicate time for specific activities and projects.

Success has twin brothers: working fast and smart. It's not enough to be fast to succeed in life. A Cheetah can run at seventy mph, reaching that speed in three seconds, yet it is an endangered creature. Working hard comes to us quite intuitively but it's not enough. I've also learned over the years that people who tend to be disorganized waste significant time they cannot recover. To be productive, you must be organized. If you are not organized yet—dealing with clutter in your life (mentally or physically) and in need of tidying up—consider techniques like the ones highlighted in the 2014 best-seller *The Life Changing Magic of Tidying Up: The Japanese Art of Decluttering and Organizing* by Marie Kondo. The phenomenon behind these organizational principles generated much interest—from articles and commentaries to a hit show on Netflix.

Let's go back to the topic at hand: How do we work smarter?

How can we avoid wasting time? Follow what I call the 6D Rule daily to make productive use of your time. This is an easy-to-use framework I came up with after years of experimentation on the corporate side, juggling countless meetings, emails, and various demands using different time management techniques. Here is how it works:

6D DAILY MANAGEMENT

	MAKING A DECISION	TAKING ACTION	SHARING INFORMATION
High ENERGY ⬆ Low ENERGY	**DECIDE**	**DRIVE**	**DISTRIBUTE**
	DELAY	**DEFLECT**	**DELEGATE**

From the moment we start each day, we are faced with numerous demands, requests, and expectations coming at full speed on our mobile devices, through emails or phone calls, or people coming to you in person. These demands typically relate to now, if not yesterday, so you often feel behind at the very same moment you are being made aware of them. They can quickly add up and become overwhelming distractions that cannot be easily avoided. Fair or not, this is your reality and you must deal with it.

To make every day a productive day, one can think about these incoming activities in three buckets: 1) a decision might be required; 2) an action might need to be taken; or 3) some information ought to be shared. As you consider each one, you must decide the level of time and energy you are allowing yourself to apply, based on the importance and urgency of each activity.

Decide or delay: If you are to make a decision, you must either decide on the spot, or delay making that decision until you have more information or need to further reflection. Either way, you must decide quickly and move on to the next one. For example, you might receive a text asking you to jump on a call the next day. You can immediately confirm or decline it, or delay responding until you have better visibility of your calendar.

Drive or deflect: If an action is required, you must decide to either see it through to completion or deflect it and do nothing. If it's an email, you can simply decide to delete it and move on. For example, you may be asked to provide a point of view on a topic. You might decide to contribute your perspective and drive the discussion. Or, you might simply decide that the question has little merit or limited value to you and simply ignore it by deflecting. If you take action, apply yourself fully. You probably won't have time to fix it later or redo it.

Distribute or delegate: If the activity is based on information that is of tangible value, it can either be distributed to the right individuals, or delegated to others for them to act. For example, someone might ask for an updated sales report. You might decide to respond by distributing the information to all concerned parties or ask someone else who is better positioned to fulfill the request to take on the responsibility of sharing this information.

> "*It's not enough to be busy. So are the ants. What are we busy about?*"

HENRY DAVID THOREAU
American essayist, poet, philospher

In these cases, you are deciding what level of energy is required and how much time you are willing to dedicate to each activity. By doing so, you are focusing on what matters most to you, what is more likely to move you forward, and what is most urgent. Some refer to this as the 80/20 or 70/30 rule, where the majority of personal or professional outcomes come only from a small portion of your daily activities. Not everything is important or urgent. Assuming you make the right decisions along the way, you are making time work harder and better for you.

BECOME A "FREAKING AWESOME" TIME MASTER
I like to think about time as a universal equalizer. We are all equal in our ability to manage time more efficiently. There are many

techniques for effective time management worth considering, and many resources to guide you along the way.

My advice is this: try getting up by five a.m. and see how you do. Try getting up by six a.m. and see if it works better. If it works for you, then stay with it. If not, simply pick a daily routine that does. Either way, go to bed every night with a stress-free spirit and wake up with a clear mind.

Stick to a regular, predictable schedule whenever possible. Avoid making too many exceptions, or your life will become one. Give yourself plenty of time to rest so you don't burn both ends of the candle. I did this in the early part of my career, working very long days to make up for the lack of technique. Resting is not a luxury, but a necessity. However, when you are on, be on. Invest in yourself.

One of my favorite techniques is called the "5-hour rule," where you set aside at least an hour every work day—effectively five hours a week—to read, reflect, meditate, learn, and take notes. In some ways, by committing to read *Success Freak* in seven days, you are well under way to apply this technique to your current lifestyle. We never fail to upgrade our computers or phones, but we often fail to

DON'T PLEASE EVERYBODY. SAYING NO TO SOMETHING IS SAYING YES TO SOMETHING ELSE.

upgrade ourselves. Read and learn a new skill every day. Many high-profile individuals have been known to practice this rule—like businessman, investor, author, and television personality Mark Cuban—who reads more than three hours a day. Whether it's one hour or three hours a day, whether you are reading a book or mediating, reserve time in your life to think outside of your everyday box to gain perspective. You may want to try a few tools and resources and see what works best for you. You can use online resources like Wunderlist, Todoist, Remember The Milk, the classic Franklin Planners (or various planning pads), or even your default to-do list app on your smartphone to manage all your activities and priorities.

Productivity consultant, David Allen, wisely says: "Your mind is for having ideas, not holding them," suggesting that our mind should be free of to-do lists that consume too much mental energy. His "get things done" approach is five steps: 1) collect what has your attention; 2) process what it means; 3) put it where it belongs; 4) review frequently; and 5) simply do. Clear your mind so it's free to problem solve and be creative instead.

Most of us are visual and favor techniques that make consumption of data far easier. Consider color-coding your daily activities on a calendar to track your time and proactively monitor where you spend it. For example, you might want to label your travel time between appointments or activities in one color. I assign colors to the most significant time activities in my life: work-related (meetings, computer time, getting things done, etc.); health (exercising, taking care of health-related situations for me or others in my life); personal time (reading, learning, family/friends); paying bills; running errands, etc. This is something I do regularly to quickly visualize my activities and make sure I have enough prep time scheduled. You may want to color your time off or holidays in a separate color. You can then quickly get a visual idea of where your time is going. Look for large blocks where there is disproportionate allocation of time and decide if this is right for you. Are you spending enough time with your family? Are you dedicating enough time to exercise regularly? Is your time allocation consistently aligned with your top priorities? If not, it might be time to course-correct and adjust your calendar. Most software calendars like Microsoft Outlook offer the capability to view your calendar as a mosaic of activities. Many smartphone calendar apps also allow color-coding.

Keep in mind that there are 1,440 minutes in a given day. Assuming you sleep eight hours a night on average, that leaves you with 960 minutes to accomplish wonders: family and relationships, work, meals, exercising, chores, educational activities, and more.

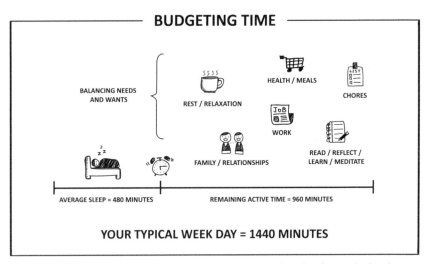

BUDGETING TIME

BALANCING NEEDS AND WANTS

REST / RELAXATION

HEALTH / MEALS

CHORES

JOB
WORK

FAMILY / RELATIONSHIPS

READ / REFLECT / LEARN / MEDITATE

AVERAGE SLEEP = 480 MINUTES

REMAINING ACTIVE TIME = 960 MINUTES

YOUR TYPICAL WEEK DAY = 1440 MINUTES

Prioritize well. I've met so many individuals with high potential that didn't know how to prioritize and ended up wasting time and effort on trivial activities. What a tragedy. We can accomplish so much more when we make better use of our time. Irish actor and playwright, Dion Boucicault, used to say jokingly that "Men talk of killing time, while time quietly kills them." Time kills us when we are not turning it into an asset. There is no time to kill if you are to succeed at whatever you set your mind to achieve. We often wish to be born with extraordinary talent when all we really need is extraordinarily hard work and good time-management skills to thrive.

Finally, time is one of our valuable resources, yet we often abuse it or waste it. We often treat time as a commodity. Time is incredibly valuable because, as is anything of great value, it is limited in supply. By the end of this chapter, you will have invested approximately sixty minutes into your future—but that investment won't pay off until you start making important decisions that will change how you effectively use your time. Become your own time master by practicing these skills. If you master your time, you will ultimately master your life.

EXERCISE #5

CONSIDER THIS EXERCISE TO COMPLETE THIS CHAPTER.
WRITE DOWN ANSWERS TO THE
FOLLOWING QUESTIONS:

1. How much of your time do you consider to be productive?
What would you like it to be?

_____

_____

_____

_____

_____

2. What regular activities in your life do you consider to be significant
time-wasters that could be easily discontinued or replaced?

_____

_____

_____

_____

3. What would an ideal day look like to get what you need accomplished
while maintaining a healthy work/life balance?

_____

4. Are you able to practice delayed gratification for important things in your life, and if so, name one example?

5. What tools or resources can you leverage now to make your time significantly more productive and more efficient?

DAY FIVE, SKILL FIVE
ACTION PLAN

Now that you have completed the exercise section and have reflected on ways you can build this new skill, it's time to act. Here are seven specific actions you must take to immediately apply what you've learned in this chapter:

CHALLENGE FIVE:
ACCOMPLISH MORE BY MASTERING
THE EFFECTIVE USE OF TIME

☐ Remember, success is not a nine-to-five commitment. Start your day early or finish it late. Make the best use of the limited time you have.

☐ Focus on being productive with your time. Use productivity tools and apps to assist. Work smart, not just hard, for better results.

☐ Start removing time-wasters or energy-killers—tasks, people, thoughts, activities—from your life that are counterproductive, drain you or steer you away from your end goal.

☐ Visualize your calendar to keep a balanced schedule. Organize your tasks into short, timed intervals spaced out by short breaks so you stay energized and on task.

☐ Think about long-term objectives while handling short-term tasks. Embrace delayed gratification, but only for worthy purposes.

☐ Follow the 6D rule daily. Adjust your energy level to your priorities.

☐ Become a professional time master. Turn time into a powerful asset, not a commodity. Remind those around you to respect your time.

DAY SIX, SKILL SIX

"Let me tell you the secret that led me to my goal. My strength lies solely in my tenacity."

LOUIS PASTEUR
French Chemist & Microbiologist

THE HEART OF A WATER BEAR

DAY SIX, SKILL SIX

Demonstrate unmatched dedication and resilience

ESTIMATED READING TIME: TWENTY MINUTES

ESTIMATED EXERCISE TIME: FIFTEEN MINUTES

 Are you a quitter or a fighter? Let's face it, there's a natural born fighter in every single one of us. But what kind of fighter are you? Could you, against all odds, withstand the worst nature could throw at you and survive freezing temperatures, radiation exposure, complete dehydration, supreme heat contact, and even a vacuum of space without any oxygen? Seems impossible, right? I thought so, too. However, one species can withstand the most severe and destructive environmental conditions known to mankind. It's time the two of you meet.

These remarkable microscopic animals are called tardigrades, also known as "water bears." The secret of the water bear's survival skills can be found in its ability to evolve—acquiring characteristics as its environment changes. Technically speaking, the 1.5mm long water bear systematically repairs its damaged DNA while experiencing serious trauma in a way that's enviable.

BEING PERSISTENT IS ALWAYS A PERSONAL DECISION.

Although we as humans may never achieve the status of most resilient species, we can look at what scientists have learned about what makes this animal so invincible and see how it might apply to human beings. Louisiana State University business professor Leon C. Megginson once claimed, referencing Darwin's *Origin of Species*, that the species that are known to survive are not the strongest or the most intelligent as one might expect. To survive, one must be highly responsive to change. Scientists have come to a similar conclusion about water bears. What appears to be the heart of their strength is their ability to adapt to ever-changing, difficult environments—as well as their innate resilience.

BE WILLING TO ADAPT AND EVOLVE RAPIDLY

Success has many close friends, but does not possess a better, or more personal, companion than resilience or grit. What does that entail? Resilience is about working strenuously toward significant challenges while sustaining effort and attention over time, despite adversity, plateaus in progress, and failures. Everyone wants to be successful until, of course, they see what it takes. There are too many reasons to quit, turn around, cut losses; too many excuses to give up. Most people don't want to do what it takes to push their limits.

Babe Ruth, the legendary professional baseball player whose career spanned twenty-two long seasons, earning him the nickname "The Sultan of Swat," perhaps summarized it best when he claimed that it's impossible to beat someone who never gives up. He would know. Ruth was fiercely competitive and resilient, becoming one of the greatest baseball players of all time. Even outside of the sports arena, the list of attributes of high-achieving individuals is quite long, including high IQ, emotional intelligence, charisma, self-confidence, and other qualities. All are important contributing factors. But only those who are willing to make sacrifices, stay committed, and, more importantly, stay flexible enough to adapt to new environments like a water bear, will win the race. Easier said than done, right?

I will show you how to be one of them. Being willing to change and evolve in the process is of utmost importance to build this muscle. Persistence is not to be confused with stubbornness. Donkeys and mules have the reputation of being stubborn animals, but they are clearly not at the top of the animal kingdom. I rest my case.

ACCEPT THAT PERFECT ISN'T PRETTY AND NEVER WILL BE

What do Ashton Eaton (USA, decathlete), Neymar Jr. (Brazil, soccer player), Ning Zetao (China, freestyle swimmer) and Andy Tennant (Great Britain, cyclist) have in common? For one, they know that perfection is a hard and moving target. In the heartfelt P&G Gillette "Perfect Isn't

Pretty" film featuring a never-before-heard mix of Sia's popular track "Unstoppable" for the Rio 2016 Olympic Games, the brand provided a glimpse into the athlete's Olympic training as they diligently prepared themselves for the competitive event.

The film pulls back the curtain and shines a vibrant spotlight on the grueling and extraordinary efforts that professional athletes face in their journey to Olympic excellence. The film was so inspiring to audiences that it quickly became one of the most shared videos of that year. What emotional trigger did they pull? How

MAKE SMALL EFFORTS DAY IN AND DAY OUT FOR A LARGE OUTCOME.

can we so easily relate to Olympic stars across so many sports categories? The inspiring film touched a nerve among the Gillette audience and ended up receiving major accolades. It reminded us that any noteworthy achievement requires a combination of arduous work and dedication, especially when facing adversity, painful rejections, repeat setbacks, and failures— as high performers often do. We idolize their heroic accomplishments, conveniently forgetting what it took them to get there (and keep them there). Even their prodigiously gifted peers won't reach the same level of performance. It's hard and it gets messy. In the ever-challenging world of personal and professional accomplishments, perfect is never pretty, period. Don't expect it to be easy. If it's easy, it's probably not worth it.

TEST YOUR PAIN AND FATIGUE TOLERANCE
There is no better example of perseverance than the hardest and most challenging trail race in the world, which fewer than twenty people have finished since its inception in 1986, to understand the effect of determination on one's ability to push the limits of what's possible.

I discovered the brutal indie Barkley ultramarathon in a 2014 documentary that left me in awe when I witnessed what personal qualities it took to finish the race. By the way, some years no one finishes. Listen to this: As if it wasn't challenging enough, no racer can receive any assistance. There is no aid station or markers. Each runner must follow a map provided the night prior to the event, showing the location of books that each runner must tear a page from to complete the race. The event organizers only accept forty runners each year who will face an unmarked 100-mile course, day and night, through treacherous pathways and routes, climbing and descending twice the height of Mount Everest in under sixty hours.

You are probably wondering as I did: Why do so few individuals ever complete it? What does it take to finish such a race? What qualities must the participants exhibit to have a shot at it? No matter how you cut it, this race is clearly more a test of resilience, sheer will, and absolute determination than any other endurance competition I am aware of. What is most remarkable about those who have managed to finish it is the common characteristics they all share. It's also noteworthy to mention traits many did not have. For example, I noticed that none of these remarkable individuals were professional athletes or looked like your typical special forces marine. Instead, beyond stereotypes, what they seemed to have in common was a remarkable willpower that enabled them to finish the insane 100-mile race. They had the ability to set their mind to accomplish a goal, no matter the obstacles, and stay committed to seeing it through. If you are wondering, the current Barkley Marathon record is held by Brett Maune, who finished the race in fifty-two hours, three minutes and eight seconds. Impressive, isn't it? No doubt, Brett is a Success Freak.

> "In all human affairs there are efforts, and there are results, and the strength of the effort is the measure of the result."
>
> **JAMES ALLEN**
> *British writer*

Now consider your own goals and ask yourself: How badly do I want it? Am I willing to wake up early and sacrifice a bit of my social life to find the time to train or practice repeatedly? Am I willing to face the pain and still choose to push forward until my goal is achieved? In the end, it's the ability to deal with stressful or uncertain situations, combined with the aptitude to tolerate some fatigue and pain over an extended period, that separates those who go on and those who give up. Most people go through life looking for maximum comfort and minimize any type of pain. We are spoiled. We are protected. We often choose the easy path, instead of the right path. When the pressure or pain is too great, we slow down or even stop in our tracks. I am not suggesting that successful individuals are all masochists who enjoy putting themselves into painful situations, but if you are unwilling to sacrifice your comfort to achieve your goal, it's unlikely that you will arrive at the desired outcome.

I was privileged to be raised as a cyclist in France and competed there for five years in my teen. I have to thank my dad, Yves, for it. He was a cyclist fanatic and signed me up as soon as I was of age to compete. 100-mile long races, and the training required prior—no matter the

LIFE IS NOT EASY: TOUGH LUCK!

weather conditions—taught me early on to "suck it up." I built up a tolerance for pain and resistance and that ability led me to deal with less than comfortable situations in my life. No one can realize remarkable feats without a healthy dose of discomfort and a right measure of commitment and dedication. Remind yourself that if you are experiencing fatigue or pain, everyone else is as well. Know yourself, know your limits, and push them slightly, again and again. Redouble your efforts, do not succumb to mediocrity, and you can bounce back from whatever setback you may experience. The right mindset will set you apart.

UNLEASH THE POWER OF POSITIVE THINKING (ESPECIALLY WHEN TIMES ARE TOUGH)

How do we bounce back from the trauma of everyday life and find the energy to keep going? To succeed at anything you take on, you must show absolute resilience to keep moving ahead even when confronted with the toughest obstacles and roadblocks. Unless you live in a cocoon, shielded from reality, life is far from being easy. It takes your breath away, literally.

Success is mostly about the right mindset. Expect plenty of curveballs. This is where a positive mindset makes the difference between tenacity and indecision, being hopeful and being determined, being optimistic and being a positive thinker. It's easy to think positively when we have moderate success, support, and access to resources. The real test is staying positive when we don't. In my mind, positive thinking goes far beyond optimism and draws from confidence, vision, and certainty. When we combine these powerful forces together, we turn ideas into

SOON ENOUGH, THE UNRELENTING PURSUIT OF YOUR GOALS WILL PAY OFF.

actions, and these actions into results. Positive thinking is a sort of fuel that stimulates our minds and bodies while propelling us forward. How can we encourage positive thinking at all times and in all circumstances?

We must first focus on the positive and brush away doubts,

hesitations, and fears. For example, someone might conclude that he or she could have started sooner on a project. That's clearly a negative thought. Instead, they should consider that starting later on this project allowed them to become wiser, and better prepared to go after their dream. In other words, the time wasn't wasted. It was invested in getting them ready for what's coming next and increased their chances of success as a result. That's a positive thought. Actually, that's two. And this is exactly what you need to focus on to keep you energized and motivated. In your darkest moments, close your eyes and listen to that inner voice whispering, "I am unstoppable." That voice knows you best.

 **LIVE BY THE "NO MATTER WHAT" MOTTO**
Attitude is everything. Leading organizations hire for attitude and train for aptitude. Why? Because they cannot realistically train employees for attitude. It's too hard and it's bound to fail. If it cannot be learned, how can we at least bring it to life?

First, try to refrain from using words like "would" and "could" when describing your goals. We think to ourselves: "I had to quit early. I would have finished if I had the right resources at my fingertips," or "I could have succeeded if I had prioritized, but way too much is going on right now in my personal life." You get the idea. We dispense these words as if they are facts and not excuses. Instead, we must take 100 percent responsibility for how far we are from our goals and commitment to them.

We may not be able to control our circumstances or what life may have in store for us, but we have absolute control about how we react to the circumstance. A small part of life is what happens to us, but the larger, more intriguing part of life is what we choose to do about it. If we do not take responsibility we cannot learn, grow, and challenge ourselves; we cannot reach our goals. Taking accountability is the first step toward being tenacious and resilient, because it's accepting that we have sole control over our destiny. Don't stare at closed doors. Instead, break them down or look for open ones.

Has anyone ever told you that something was "impossible?" Did you make the mistake of believing them? Impossible kills dreams and can be paralyzing, holding us back. By revealing tough and often overlooked everyday struggles, we learn to appreciate the muscles that must be built and the skills that must be learned to make the impossible possible. We can't do so without shifting our mindset and resetting our perspective on what we think is within our reach. Listen to your inner voice guide you in the most difficult times, when quitting seems the most reasonable option.

Be unreasonable, always. Seeing what is possible requires a vision of what the outcome is, and a willingness to accept failure after failure, not letting them discourage you from reaching that goal. It's easier said than done. Most people start a task or a project with a set number of attempts they are willing to try before calling it quits. It would be crazy to do otherwise. Yet, those who defy common sense and refuse to quit are those who accomplish greatness. Typically, that number of attempts is determined by the following: How important is that goal to us? How painful is each failed attempt? What's our likelihood of success? The least important task, that also happens to be painful or embarrassing, is likely to be attempted only once or twice before the decision is made to give up. The more important the task, even if failed attempts prove to be painful, are often worth the risk.

> *"With ordinary talent and extraordinary perseverance, all things are attainable."*
>
> ———
>
> ## SIR THOMAS FOWELL BUXTON
> *English politician, abolitionist and social reformer*

"I COULD EITHER WATCH IT HAPPEN OR BE A PART OF IT."
Imagine for a second that you were born far away from the US, in the southernmost country of the eastern hemisphere. Imagine your parents got divorced when you were only 9 years old and, to make matters worse, you had a tough childhood. You were severely bullied to the point of being thrown down a flight of stairs and had to go to the hospital. Now imagine yourself moving to Canada right before turning eighteen. Then, at age twenty-four, you move to California to begin a PhD in applied physics and materials science at one of the most prestigious schools in the US, Stanford University. Fast forward a few years and now imagine that you have been at the head of some of the most exciting innovative ventures and, one day, woke up to realize you were the eightieth-wealthiest person in the world with a net worth estimated at $15.2 billion. This is not the

story of a someone willing to watch a game unfold on the side line, but rather the story of a fighter who pushed himself to his limits to decide the outcome of the game. This is the story of entrepreneur and business magnate Elon Musk.

Elon Musk is the most compelling example of grit in business today, as illustrated by how he persevered to launch his SpaceX rocket after a few failed attempts that nearly bankrupted the company. It was only on the fourth try that the mission became successful. In an interview, Scott Cameron Pelley, television reporter and correspondent for *60 Minutes* asked if the entrepreneur should consider giving up after three consecutive failures. The business maverick answered that he would rather be dead or incapacitated than give up. It's not surprising that he is the entrepreneur behind incredibly successful and daring enterprises like SpaceX corporation, SolarCity, Neuralink, Tesla, Inc., and PayPal. Musk's success is not about his personal wealth, but rather his ability to commit himself to what he loves most.

STOP; BREATHE; THINK; START OVER
Textbooks are filled with examples of scientists, entrepreneurs, activists, and athletes unwilling to quit, becoming icons of defiance, dedication, and perseverance for generations to come. This is the case of American inventor and businessman Thomas Alva Edison, who was a prolific inventor. Yet, it was his resilience that allowed him to see many of those inventions through despite countless setbacks.

This was also the case of Milton Snavely Hershey, the American confectioner who founded the Hershey Chocolate Company after three unsuccessful businesses and significant financial loss. Likewise, for British athlete Derek Redmond, who during the 1992 Olympics, tore his hamstring in the middle of a race in which he was expected to win a gold medal. He fell to the ground in pain yet, despite stretcher-bearers making their way over to him, decided to get up onto his feet and finish the race in front of 65,000 spectators who gave him a standing ovation. The stories of these Success Freaks are forever reminders of the power of discipline and grit.

> ## "That which does not kill me makes me stronger."
>
> ### FRIEDRICH NIETZSCHE
> *German philosopher and poet*

Research over the past 100 years, including recent findings by the University of Pennsylvania, University of Michigan, and the United States Military Academy of West Point, showed which qualities distinguish star performers in their respective fields. The findings demonstrated that these individuals all exhibited resilience and determination, despite apparently being less gifted than their peers. Defined as perseverance and passion for long-term goals, these qualities accounted for an average of four percent of the variance in success outcomes in one study.

A qualitative study of the development of world-class neurologists, athletes, chess players, mathematicians, and artists showed that only a few of them were regarded as prodigies by others around them. Rather, these world-class individuals worked day after day, for at least ten or fifteen years, overcoming setbacks to reach the top of their fields.

The common recipe? A strong, continued interest in their particular field, a desire to reach a high level of success in it, and a willingness to invest significant time and effort.

BUILD UP THE RESISTANCE OF A PALM TREE It's not enough to be strong to succeed in life. Some of the strongest materials can break under pressure, from lack of flexibility, or simply sinking to the bottom.

Imagine being caught in a category five hurricane with frightening winds exceeding 156 mph. Not much can survive the fury and devastating effects of this incredible phenomenon of nature. Yet, palm trees stand their ground in the toughest, most intense weather, managing to survive hurricanes, cyclones, and even tsunamis. How do they do it?

Plant ecologists discovered three distinctive features that help them survive in the harshest of conditions: 1) their large number of small roots are spread across the soil, keeping them stable; 2) the trunk grows in a radial pattern of concentric hollow cylinders, making it incredibly strong; 3) they have no large branches, but instead, large leaves with a flexible spine that can fold under pressure.

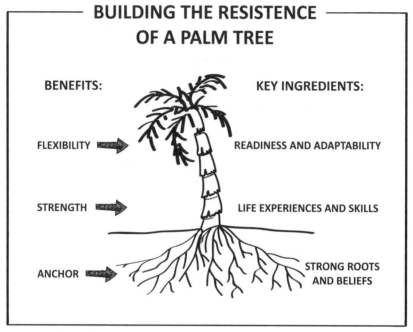

What does it mean to us? Well, to build the resistance of a palm tree, we must first build strong roots and beliefs as an anchor we can rely on when things get challenging. We must also build one layer after another of life experiences and skills that make us stronger at our core, better preparing us to handle such events. Finally, we must be clever and flexible enough to avoid excessive or pointless resistance when needing to adjust to ever-changing circumstances.

It takes extraordinary will to accomplish extraordinary things. Look carefully and you will see that greatness is inside us all. We know that the achievement of goals requires not only ability or talent but, equally important, the sustained and focused application of talent over time. Resilience is what makes some individuals try and try again when most people would have already quit. They work hard and go the extra mile. They stay on task and are diligent, staying focused. They finish whatever they begin, keep dreaming big, and do not let setbacks discourage them. Their determination can come across as stubbornness, or even insanity, to the most moderate among us. Yet, they see obstacles as tests to overcome, reinforcing their will to see things through.

Nothing easy in life is worth chasing. To become a Success Freak, you must acknowledge that being resilient is not only a skill that must be acquired, developed, and mastered, but also a prerequisite mindset to pursue and accomplish anything truly worthwhile in life.

EXERCISE #6

CONSIDER THIS EXERCISE TO COMPLETE THIS CHAPTER.
WRITE DOWN ANSWERS TO THE
FOLLOWING QUESTIONS:

1. What goals do you currently find to be impossible to reach and why?

_____

_____

_____

_____

_____

2. How many failed attempts do you feel are reasonable before finding it acceptable "to throw in the towel"?

_____

_____

_____

_____

_____

3. What is the maximum level of pain you have ever sustained pursuing a goal? How important was that goal to you? What did you learn from it?

_____

4. When was the last time someone told you something was impossible? How did you react?

5. When you hear "no matter what", which sacrifices do you feel are necessary? Are you willing to make them?

ACTION PLAN

Now that you have completed the exercise section and have reflected on ways you can build this new skill, it's time to act. Here are seven specific actions you must take to immediately apply what you've learned in this chapter:

CHALLENGE SIX:
DEMONSTRATE UNMATCHED DEDICATION AND RESILIENCE

☐ When things get tough, stay the course. Remember that perfect isn't pretty for anyone and that it takes extraordinary will to accomplish extraordinary things.

☐ Acknowledge that, in the pursuit of goals, pain is inevitable. However, suffering—which is different than pain—is optional. The path to success is not a gentle one.

☐ When you are ready to quit, don't. Listen to your heart instead, not to your muscles, reactions, or self esteem. Keep your eyes on the prize.

☐ Turn every negative thought into a positive one. Remind yourself that nothing of purpose is ever easy. The harder the journey, the more rewarding it will be.

☐ Listen to your inner voice when the path is unclear. Stay away from dream killers or anyone that feels your goals are impossible; show them otherwise.

☐ Like a palm tree, rely on the roots and beliefs you built over the years; remain flexible, but determined, in the face of adversity.

☐ Don't start the day hoping to accomplish something. Just make it happen. Stop using the words "trying" or "wishing" altogether.

DAY SEVEN, SKILL SEVEN

"Let your passion take you on a lifelong journey of discovery and fulfillment."

BRUNO GRALPOIS

French American Entrepreneur & Author

BURNING WITH PASSION

DAY SEVEN, SKILL SEVEN

Pursue a life of burning passion and purpose

ESTIMATED READING TIME: TWENTY-TWO MINUTES

ESTIMATED EXERCISE TIME: FIFTEEN MINUTES

 In 1975, a woman under a hairdryer at a beauty parlor watched the owner's son, a college student, seated nearby. That struggling student happened to have flunked out of college with a 1.7 grade point average, and was considering joining the army, unsure of where life was going to take him next. Every time he looked up, the woman was staring at him in the eye, but he didn't know who she was. She suddenly asked for a pen, as she had a prophecy to share: he would travel the world and speak to millions of people. These words would stay with him throughout his career— the young student being

Oscar-award-winning actor, Denzel Washington who, ultimately, earned a B.A. in Drama and Journalism from Fordham University two years later.

The now widely acclaimed director and producer, and recipient of three Golden Globe awards, a Tony Award, and two Academy Awards, shared his personal story at the Dillard University commencement ceremony on May 9, 2015, hoping to inspire others to dream big, make changes, follow their passions, and set goals. Washington said: "Don't be afraid to go outside the box. Don't be afraid to think outside the box. Don't be afraid to fail big, to dream big, but remember, dreams without goals, are just dreams." Washington knows a thing or two about the often-convoluted ways we discover our true calling in life.

Washington discovered his passion after participating in a staff talent show for campers while working as creative arts director at an overnight summer camp in Lakeville, Connecticut. A colleague suggested he try acting and the rest is history. Denzel Washington is a talented actor, director, producer and a Success Freak. Passion is all around us, even though we may not always see it, and it is a powerful energy and catalyst. We can hear it in people's voices as they share with us what they do, what they think, what they dream of. Likewise,

LOVE WHAT YOU DO. DO WHAT YOU LOVE.

we can hear intense emotion and enthusiasm in our own voice when we speak to the fire inside of us. Passion is a door to your success; find your door and push it wide open.

DISCOVER WHAT MAKES YOUR HEART SING
"I am passionate about helping people in need."
"I am passionate about learning foreign languages."
"I am passionate about writing fiction."
"I am passionate about protecting the environment."

What drives you? Some people know their calling with absolute certainty. Others are still seeking what makes their heart sing. If you are still looking, consider traveling, reading, coaching, mentoring, going to school, or conducting self-assessments. But if you do know your calling, do you have a statement, or way of articulating to yourself and others, what you are passionate about? Are you excited when you read it out loud? My personal passion statement is the following: Through conceptualizing ideas, writing, and speaking about self-improvement (the HOW), my passion is to positively contribute to enriching the lives of others, (the WHAT) as it brings me joy and fulfillment, and allows me to learn from others (the WHY).

Although there are no set rules, I believe a passion statement must be authentic, clear, convey what you care about most, and provide a long-term perspective on your overarching aspirations as an individual and member of society. It may combine personal and career ambitions. It must be based on the idea that anything is possible. Don't be intimated, this passion statement is yours. It can be changed as often as you wish, at any time. It supports you in making choices that propel you forward, toward your future life.

Passion is indeed a fire, a sort of burning flame that acts as a compass and source of unlimited positive energy, forward motion, and growth. Sadly, some of us never find that flame,

DON'T LIVE WITHOUT PASSION. IT'S THE FUEL OF A GREAT LIFE.

or worse, let it slowly die by giving up on our personal dreams and ambitions. As any source of energy, the size of the flame is proportional to the amount of energy it produces. The more passionate we are about something, the more energy we produce and capitalize on. What separates the greatest achievers from the rest of the world? Passion is clearly one of the most important ingredients to living a successful life.

Have you heard of a success story from someone who wasn't truly passionate about what they did? I can't think of one. Neither can you, I bet. Some may argue that exceptional achievement does not require passion and that—because passion indirectly leads to hours of study and practice— when combined with natural ability, it may create outstanding results. Can we be so incredibly talented that, even without passion, it can lead to greatness? I seriously doubt it, as the pursuit of greatness often requires more than talent. Perhaps this is what German-born theoretical physicist Albert Einstein meant when he said, "I have no special talents. I am only passionately curious."

GIVE WINGS TO WHAT YOU LOVE

Why is passion so essential? In prior chapters, I spoke to the importance of developing essential skills to become amazingly successful. Passion is the connective tissue between the skillsets, and therefore the most important. In the most troubled times, we reach deep inside our hearts to rediscover our true purpose and keep the flame alive. There is no greater evidence of people burning with passion than those who receive a lifetime achievement, or other significant award, by an organization of their peers—whether in science, literature, sports, peace, economics, art—recognizing individuals for their contribution to a particular project, or over a whole career dedicated to what they love.

Do what you love in life and you will have the energy to fight every obstacle, bounce back, stay focused and determined, think and act differently. Without passion, it all falls apart and frankly, it loses its purpose. This is probably why the word "passion" comes from a Greek verb meaning "to suffer." A burning, borderline obsessive, desire allows one to sustain pain, disappointments, setbacks, and anything that could get in the way of the vision. Of course, pushed to an extreme, we can become slaves to our passion, especially if it starts to have control over us. We can lose the perspective and balance often required to use our passion as a source of positive, as opposed to destructive, energy. We fear defeat and disillusions, as the mind can play tricks, but a genuine heart does not submit to fear.

Although we understand what passion is, at least conceptually, putting it into everyday practice presents some inherent challenges. Confronted with the social and economic reality and pressures of everyday life, how do we think and live boldly? How do we live passionately without falling into the trap of compromise or being too practical? Can we be reasonable and incredibly passionate at the same time? I honestly don't think so. Excessive reason is no friend to a passionate life.

> *"Nothing great in the world has been accomplished without passion."*
>
> ---
>
> ## GEORG WILHELM FRIEDRICH HEGEL
> *German philosopher*

SEARCH UNTIL YOU FIND IT, OR UNTIL IT FINDS YOU

"Do what you love. Love what you do." This popular advice is given to young adults considering what studies or careers to pursue when facing a crossroads. It seems like obvious, sound advice, yet many people scratch their heads, uncertain of the path they should choose. Why is that? Do we always know what we are passionate about? Is that something we discover early on in our childhood? What should we expect? The reality is that some people struggle through life to find their true passion. They develop interests in various topics or hobbies which come and go, as we all do. But finding one's real lifetime passion can prove to be difficult. It requires a curiosity to explore the world and find one's place in it. Being curious means asking many questions about the "why" and "how," and exploring, listening, and embracing life's opportunities with an open mind.

When you align your passion with your profession, you find your "*raison d'être.*" A similar concept in Japan, known as "*Ikigai,*" states that everyone has an *ikigai*, a reason for being. The term ikigai compounds two Japanese words: *iki* meaning "life; alive," and *kai* meaning a "value; effect; result or usefulness." It sits at the intersection of what we love, what we are good at, what we can be paid for, and what the world needs.

We may feel that we are passionate about too many things or that we can't point to anything specific. Being passionate often means that we are obsessed with a single thing, to the exclusion of everything else. It can be terribly consuming. Unless we develop a certain level of consciousness, self-awareness, and deliberateness, we cannot make what we love the center of our lives.

A passion can still be dormant, ready to be discovered. How do we find out what we are truly passionate about? Let's be frank, if you don't intuitively know the answer to that question, you haven't found it yet. It's all right, keep searching until you do. Realize that you might discover your passion in life the same way you meet your soulmate—when you least expect to.

Some are lucky enough to find their passion early on in life. American professional boxer, Muhammad Ali, discovered the boxing ring after threatening to find and fight the thief of his bicycle—a gift from his parents for his twelfth birthday—to a local policeman who also happened to be a boxing instructor. American entrepreneur and Microsoft co-founder, Bill Gates, discovered his passion for computer science after being exposed to a teletype terminal provided to school students.

Others have discovered and pursued their vocation later in life. Dutch Post-Impressionist painter, Vincent van Gogh, decided to become an artist at age twenty-seven after working as an art dealer, teacher, and missionary. American chef and television personality Julia Child held many jobs—copywriter, typist, research assistant. Child moved to Paris at age thirty-six and was almost fifty years old when she managed to find a publisher for her famous cookbook and soon to be best-seller *Mastering the Art of French Cooking*. Italian Classical Tenor, Andrea Bocelli who became completely blind at age 12, completed law school and became a court-appointed lawyer. The internationally-acclaimed recording artist and singer-songwriter performed evenings in piano bars during college but only started a career in music at age thirty-four.

It's never too late to discover your passion, the key is to be open-minded and curious. Be open to trying new activities and meeting new people. Travel and see the world; pick up a book;

attend a lecture. Consider taking a class on something you've always wanted to try. Most importantly, listen to your heart, as it will guide you to your passion. In the end, it's not WHAT we did in life that matters, it's WHY we did it.

> *"The two most important days*
> *in your life are the day you*
> *are born and the day you*
> *found out why."*
>
> ### MARK TWAIN
> *American writer*

LIVING YOUR DREAM VS. DREAMING YOUR LIFE

 Passion is addictive. Try telling someone passionate to stop what they are doing. They can't give it up. It's part of who they are, what brings them joy, peace, and a sense of fulfilment. Some are lucky enough to combine their passion with their professional occupation. Others work to live, their life taking meaning only after they finish their work day. Those who effectively make a living out of their passion know that the alternative is not really living, but surviving. Is your life today what you want it to be? What

makes you smile? What activity makes you lose sight of time? Ask yourself: If I didn't need to make a living, what would I do with my time? The answers to these questions will help you find what you love.

When we are passionate about our professional occupation, we are more satisfied and more capable of handling stress and obstacles. We are less likely to hold back or be mindful of the time and energy we invest. This leads to psychological wellbeing and a sense of fulfilment.

UNLEASH THE PASSION IN YOUR LIFE. LIVE YOUR DREAM.

We first must identify pivotal times in our lives when our decisions will have significant implications. Pivotal times include what we choose to study, what topics we invest ourselves in, what advice we ignore or follow, what internships we pursue, what role model we choose, what first job we seek, and the list goes on. These are pivotal moments because our choices steer us in a particular direction. Sadly, we often compromise too early, choosing a different path when the original one becomes harder than expected. For example, you need a paycheck, so you may have to accept a job that pays better, or is more stable, instead of one that is better aligned with your passions. Changing course becomes increasingly difficult, and we find ourselves stuck in a life that is less fulfilling and, in the long term, only leads to frustrations and discontent. Some individuals are unwilling to compromise, and they stay firmly committed to their passion. It takes sacrifice and patience. It takes perseverance as well. The roadblocks and setbacks are certain. For those living passionate lives, there is only one path they find acceptable. For them, dreams don't come true, they are true.

Consider the following conceptual matrix below. The "passion" matrix is divided into four quadrants and is organized around two main axes:

The commitment level: short-term or "casual" (e.g. a few months or years like a temporary job or a new hobby) or long-term or "committed" (e.g. many years like a lifelong career or vocation);

The type of commitment: personal (e.g. hobbies and vocations with zero to low earning potential) or professional (e.g. jobs and careers with medium to high earning potential).

The matrix establishes that the greater the ability to align and combine long-term personal and professional commitments, the greater the chances to live a life of purpose and passion. In other words, the individuals who successfully combine personal and professional interests get paid to do what they love. I call them "passion burners."

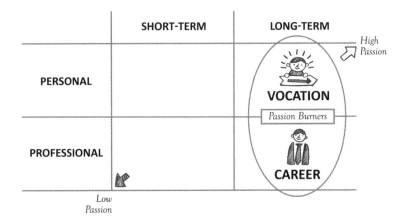

This is what many of us aspire to become.

Some people hold various jobs, often on a temporary basis, so they can afford to wholly pursue their passion. I call them "passion dreamers," as they have yet to become established in a career doing what they love. If they did, it would be a dream come true. This is the aspiring actor bussing tables at night to afford to attend auditions during the day, their real vocation.

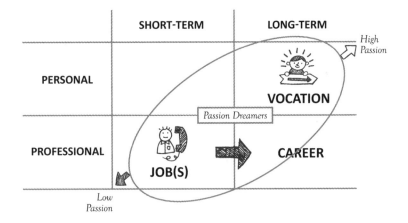

Some people have committed themselves for the long-run to a profession but also have one or several hobbies on the side. These hobbies fulfill their short-term interests, typically after work or on weekends. I call them "passion seekers," as they have yet to find a true, burning vocation. This is where many people find themselves, pursuing a career in a profession they may enjoy but have little to no long-term affinity for. They rotate through hobbies. "Passion seekers" never had the opportunity to find what they love or let themselves be consumed by their passion.

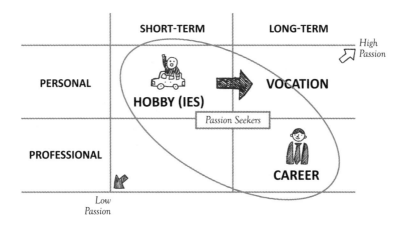

The last group is called "passion wasters," for those people jump from job to job, from hobby to hobby, never committing themselves to a craft, and never finding their real passion. For those individuals, finding what they love is the first important step in the process of reaching their "ikigai." That might involve discovering new hobbies and pursuing new interests until they find their true passion, subsequently looking for relevant professional opportunities.

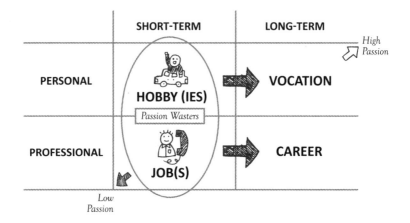

DON'T LEARN TO LOVE WHAT YOU DO;
LEARN TO DO WHAT YOU LOVE

We all want to be "passion burners," fusing our career with our life vocation. When you do, your everyday job is filled with excitement, and Monday suddenly sets a positive tone for the week instead of feeling like Doomsday or a day to survive.

Slow down and reflect on these important choices, and what it takes to find yourself in the right circumstances. Listen to your heart and intuition. Your inner voice will tell you if you are choosing the right path both personally and professionally. Life is about making some compromises. But do not compromise yourself or your dreams.

Hollywood comedian Jim Carrey, who's known for his highly energetic slapstick performances, found his purpose in his late twenties. At his commencement address to Maharishi University of Management's class of 2014, he admitted that after spending a decade as a professional comedian, at the age twenty-eight, Carrey realized that the purpose of his life had always been to free people from concern. Carrey found his purpose doing exactly what he loved, after seeing others fail at what they didn't want. He acknowledged that his father could have been a great comedian if only he believed in himself. Instead, Carrey's father made a conservative choice and got a safe job as an accountant. Carrey was only twelve years old when his father was let go from that safe job and the family struggled to survive financially, an experience the actor never forgot. Carrey admitted that he learned many lessons from his father, not the least of which was that you can fail at what you don't want, so you might as well take a chance on doing what you love.

Learn to do what you love instead of learning to love what you do; think long term; and, finally, look for the signs. When your passion is calling you, signs always appear along the way. Don't ignore them. When everything else is in flux, let purpose be your personal guide. Carrey went on to say: "Your job is not to figure out how it's going to happen for you, but to open the door in your head. And when the door opens in real life, just walk through it. And don't worry if you miss your cue, because there's always a door opening. They keep opening."

> "*Passion is the genesis of genius.*"
> ─────
> ## GALILEO GALILEI
> *Italian astronomer, physicist and engineer*

MAKE THE TIME TO TURN A PURPOSEFUL LIFE INTO A HAPPY ONE

Would you rather have a happy or meaningful life? This is a question everyone should ask themselves, because it will profoundly impact the way they go through life and the decisions they make at major intersections. The pursuit of happiness is a topic that continues to captivate audiences around the world. We wish people around us a "happy Monday" or "happy Friday." We want to be happy at any cost, even though we often struggle to define what happiness is.

The definition of "happiness" on Wikipedia is the result of 6,000 edits by over 3,000 users over a fourteen-year period. Success is often thought of as a means to pursue happiness. Yet meaning proves to be a far more powerful goal. A meaningful life channels our passion as an energy source. The reality of meaning is that it's often characterized by effort, pain, and struggle. However, when life circumstances become difficult, we can rely on meaning to get us energized and moving. We must focus on things that make our life more worthwhile and purposeful. Do not give up on your dreams. Become what you dream.

Alternatively, the pursuit of happiness without meaning or passion can leave many empty and alone. In *The Power of Meaning: Crafting a Life That Matters,* author Emily Esfahani Smith argues that there are many untapped sources of meaning within reach. An Australian professor of neurology and psychiatry at the University of Vienna Medical School, and an Holocaust survivor, Viktor Emil Frankl spoke of his Auschwitz concentration camp experience in *Man's Search for Meaning,* inviting readers to identify a personal purpose to feel positive about and to question life, daily and hourly, by doing what is right. Frankl's work is hugely inspiring, offering a unique perspective about humanity, survival, and the meaning of life. To find happiness, we must be good, do good, and live a life of purpose.

DECLARE AND SHARE YOUR PASSION WITH OTHERS

Passion can spread like a virus. Once unleashed, it's unstoppable. Have you heard someone speak passionately about what they love, only to feel your heart pumping and excitement level increase? This is natural. When we experience positive emotions like inspiration, we immediately feel energized. We can also feel other people's passion—the energy practically bursting out of their pores, eyes lit up, their faces and hands animated.

This is why Success Freaks not only burn with passion, but

they light others on fire by sharing what they love most. They are charismatic, creating forums, forming groups, sharing and collaborating with others. They seek to inform, educate, and inspire their audience. Have you listened to passion burners speak at TED about topics like biology, astronomy, alternative energy, driverless cars, gender equality, illness, performance arts, and so on? Notice how they spread their passion so brilliantly? You find yourself wanting to learn more about a topic that until now, you had little interest in. In the fall of 2012, *TED Talks* celebrated its one billionth video view, a huge success for the non-profit dedicated to spreading ideas by those who have successfully found ways to pursue their passions.

SET YOUR GOALS, DEVOTE YOURSELF AND FEEL ALIVE.

Lone Success Freaks are exceptionally rare. Every day that we take on the world, we leave footprints for others to follow. We are natural born leaders. Professor Emeritus in psychology at the University of California Davis, Dean Keith Simonton, conducted a research project scouring biographical documents for mentions of relationships among accomplished scientists like Isaac Newton and artists like Michelangelo (2,026 and 772 documents, respectively), and found that within each field there was a web of connections. These connections included friends, mentors, collaborators, associates, admirers, and rivals. We cannot become Success Freaks in complete isolation. We need to collaborate, exchange, debate, and challenge other-minded individuals as we push ourselves to greatness.

Thankfully, the resources of the internet age are endless

when it comes to finding others who share similar passions. Try creating a Facebook page, building a blog, posting your thoughts in online communities. When we share with others, we enhance our knowledge and perspective. We deepen our interests and feed our passions.

The words of Scottish novelist Robert Louis Stevenson stick with me: "Don't judge each day by the harvest you reap, but by the seeds that you plant." Connection has never been more important. When we are isolated, we miss the type of gratification and validation we get from having relationships with those who share a common passion. You see, in some way, writing *Success Freak* was my own personal way of declaring my passion and spreading my thirst for self-improvement.

DREAM "BIG," BUT MAKE A "HUGE" DIFFERENCE

Perfection only exists in the heart of the visionary. It's what drives us to push the limits of our own abilities. Only when we dream big and burn with passion can we dedicate the effort, time, and resources to sustain the pain and setbacks often necessary to achieve our goals. Let's be frank, no worthy life achievement has ever been realized without a heavy dose of passion. Dream big and break down your dream into tangible, manageable chunks, so it doesn't stay conceptual. You don't have the skills? No problem. As long as you are passionate, you will find it in you to build the skills you need. You don't have the time? If you have a passion, you will practice patience and dedicate countless moments of your life to its pursuit. You don't have the motivation? Passion is the ultimate motivator. It provides an unlimited supply of fuel to keep your engine roaring for years to come. The best way to pursue our dreams is to move forward and never look back.

Without passion, nothing magical will ever happen. Find your passion and see it flourish within you and through others. Dedicate yourself to it, making it real through deliberate efforts and commitment. Enjoy the ride, as it might be a long one, and stay open to new journeys. Share your passion with others, pull others along, and see how it transforms your life and inspires them. Aspire to make a difference by doing what you love.

EXERCISE #7

1. What would you say is your life's purpose? Is that purpose consistently guiding your decisions?

2. What is the one thing you think about before you go to bed at night and the first thing you think about when you wake up? Stated differently, what makes your heart sing and your mind travel?

3. Ask yourself how you would live this year if it were your last? What would you spend your time doing and why? If it is different from the way you live today, what gets in the way?

4. Are you pleased with your life today? What do you feel obligated or pressured to do that brings you no real pleasure or satisfaction?

5. Are you actively collaborating and sharing your passion with others? If you could do more, what would it be?

ACTION PLAN

Now that you have completed the exercise section and have reflected on ways you can build this new skill, it's time to act. Here are seven specific actions you must take to immediately apply what you've learned in this chapter:

CHALLENGE SEVEN:
PURSUE A LIFE OF BURNING PASSION AND PURPOSE

☐ Learn what you love to do most; follow your heart; don't give up until you find it.

☐ Declare your vocation and true purpose in life with a passion statement. Use the HOW, WHAT, WHY formula to do so.

☐ Never consider "work" a dirty word again. Instead, explore ways to align your vocation with a career so you can support yourself financially.

☐ Spend most of your time, energy, and efforts on what you love. Stop doing what doesn't nourish your heart and soul. Be selective.

☐ Do not walk, run, or fly blind. Use your passion to influence important life decisions and shed light on your path to success.

☐ Feel right by doing right. Stop pretending or making excuses and choose a life of purpose. Expect happiness as an outcome, not a goal.

☐ Network with individuals who share a common passion. Communicate, collaborate, and share, making your passion contagious.

CONCLUSION

"The important thing is this: to be able at any moment to sacrifice what we are for what we could become."

———

CHARLES DU BOS
French writer and critic

CONCLUSION
KICKING ASS IN LIFE

 Ants often need to walk backwards carrying a heavy load of food. These little insects, whose simple brains, smaller than a pinhead, account for about 250,000 neurons—compared with billions in a human brain—can't see where they are going, yet they have no problem finding their way home. Research shows that these insects, which originated about 99 million years ago, can rely on their visual memories to navigate, even moving backward, which may seem counterintuitive to our logical minds. How do they do it?

Ants leverage cues, like the position of the sun in the sky, or olfactory and tactile cues to more accurately find their path. They

183

cannot, however, as human beings can, reference past experiences and use their imagination to visualize what the future might look like. Like ants, we carry a heavy load of responsibilities and get constantly disoriented by difficult events or conditions in our lives. We think we are moving in the right direction, suddenly taking turns, trying to avoid dangers, and often find ourselves getting lost or off track. If ants can navigate their way home, even backwards, so can we. I hope *Success Freak* can serve as a valuable life compass to help you find your way home. By home, I mean finding your way to an incredibly successful, meaningful, and rewarding life. A life you'll enjoy every day.

YOU DID IT!

Congratulations! You've now acquired the critical skills needed to propel yourself forward. Put down everything you've been carrying with you all these years and take a deep breath. Look at what is essential to reach your goals, face your destiny, and start marching toward it. You can use the seven skills outlined to find your desired position, check your surroundings, reorient yourself, and adjust course as needed.

Take time to process the many ways you can get more from life that are highlighted in the book. Let it sink in; process it; come back to it later. You can then resume the most fulfilling aspects of your life—getting rid of what's holding you back—using valuable advice to continue confidently along your personal route to success. The journey we started together is much more than simply following a gallery of inspiring quotes to find a shortcut to your dreams. As my friend, Success Freak, solo wilderness explorer, and award-winning photographer Daniel Fox likes to say: "We 'consume' these concepts like we consume food—without taking the time to process what they mean and entail. Every day, the web is inundated with feel-good quotes, like 'It's the journey, not the destination,' Yet, our culture is all about the destination."

To profoundly change our lives, we must do more than repaint the car or change the battery. We may need to change our means of transportation or change the destination altogether. If you are curious, have a receptive mind, and have the heart to apply yourself, there are plenty of resources and unending advice out there—books, videos, blogs, interviews, and much more. Yet the pace of change continues to accelerate, and the level of ambiguity and complexity in our lives is ever greater. What we once knew may no longer be relevant today. Things change faster than ever. Uncertainty and fear settle in and we find ourselves stuck. Yet, learning and positive change occur when we step beyond what's known or what's comfortable.

I've gone through that journey. Like you, I often doubted the outcome. I experienced setbacks as an employee, as an entrepreneur, as a writer, as a friend, as a spouse, and as a family member. I failed to see the signs right in front of my face. I wasted precious time and focused on things that didn't matter. I sometimes looked back instead of looking forward. I gave up too early. I wasn't always as defiant as I should have been. I didn't break rules that slowed me down for no valid reason. I wasn't always grateful for what I had. I didn't always listen—or listened to the wrong voices—and learned life lessons the hard way.

We are often the products of our environment, but our thirst will always be stronger than our predisposition. So, say "yes" to becoming a Success Freak. It's never too late to face your weaknesses, turn pain into greatness, and reinvent yourself. Open your mind to new possibilities and push your personal limits to the point of constructive self-examination and heightened confidence. Hope is not just a word to us; it is a way of life. We have hope because we believe in our potential.

By the time you reach this chapter, you are well under way to becoming the Success Freak you always wanted to be. Change your perspective and your job title. Be a talent creator; conquest engineer; opportunity maker. You see, success is a constant state of transition, so celebrate what you have. You must also make the necessary effort and sacrifices to become what you owe it to yourself to be.

We want to matter. We want to infuse purpose into what we do and enjoy a life of meaning and genuine passion. Success is the key. Not the kind of device that unlocks doors, but rather the type of information we must uncover to decipher a personal message hidden in each one of us. A sort of map that will guide us through setbacks and uncertainty and keep us on track. Find that key, and anything becomes possible.

"It is impossible for anyone to begin to learn that which he thinks he already knows."

EPICTETUS
Greek philosopher

FLEX YOUR SUCCESS MUSCLES

The question that was introduced at the beginning of this journey was: what do these success stories have in common? What are the key ingredients so many are eagerly searching for? We now have answers. Change always starts with a convincing case, and hopefully, you now have one.

I carefully picked the skills, through mindful practice and mental discipline, that are essential to success. They will become the operating principles that drive your decisions, actions, and attitude. Many people spend a lifetime pursuing a purpose that causes them to forge a path, concluding their life with the knowledge that they succeeded in seeing their dreams—or a good many of them—come true.

Some call it "happiness," "purpose," "fulfillment," or "life achievements." You can now join other highly-motivated individuals who have made their lives a source of inspiration to others. Their stories represent real potential; the ability of one exceptional individual to catapult ahead and move swiftly towards his or her ambitions. Think about these skills as success muscles you must work to build and strengthen. By building the correct muscles and embracing the right habits, Success Freaks like you can live more fulfilling and productive lives. Flex your success muscles daily.

FLEX

your

SUCCESS MUSCLES

THINK AND ACT
differently, living
by your own rules

CREATE
your own personal
measurement of success

BECOME
obsessively
outcome-oriented

LEARN TO FAIL SMART
and strengthen
your character

DEMONSTRATE
unmatched dedication
and resilience

ACCOMPLISH MORE
by mastering the
effective use of time

PURSUE
a life of burning passion and purpose

Every new day is another opportunity to apply these new skills and transform both your personal and professional circumstances. It doesn't end here—to the contrary, whether you mean to or not, you will soon become a role model to others. People will look up to you, because you show absolute drive and confidence. Believe me when I say that confidence is more contagious than a cold in wintertime. By building

DON'T GET LOST. THE ROAD IS THE DESTINATION.

the seven skills highlighted in this book, you'll build, and eventually master, the necessary skills to unleash the amazing "you" that has been dormant and is now awakened.

I dedicated time and effort in recent years to study remarkable individuals who acquired and built skills that proved to propel them forward to their personal success story. I've spoken to many of these Success Freaks as I wrote these chapters, and analyzed countless personal stories of achievement and defiance, as I determined the most appropriate examples to mention in this book. Each of these provided additional insight to inspire or guide you. However, the only story that really matters is the one you will be writing for yourself, using what you've learned here.

VALUABLE LESSONS LEARNED

Greatness is not just for the few; it's nothing more than one's willingness to want more and to work hard to achieve it. Here are the essential lessons we learned and the skills we developed in the seven-day *Success Freak* challenge:

CLAIM
your success

1. CLAIM YOUR SUCCESS

Are you tired of being compared to others? Or feeling pressured by those around you to meet their definition of success?

Whatever you decide to call it, you must come up with your own personal definition of success. This is the only measure that truly matters in the end. You've been conditioned to think about your success based on society's conventional wisdom, or by idealizing fame and fortune as measures of success. Yet you fail to see that you, and only you, can decide what success is. You may already be successful and don't know it, because you rely on others to tell you if you are or not. Or you feel that you must earn their approval to declare your own success. You don't need anyone's approval to declare what success is for you. Success is yours if you claim it; claim what is yours.

DARE
to be different

2. DARE TO BE DIFFERENT

Are you exhausted by being told what to do? Tired of being brainwashed day in and day out, wondering if there's a place for following your inner voice?

You've been trained to think and act like everyone else; to conform and be accepted. By doing so, your thoughts and actions might be nothing more than average. You disagree? Good. That's the point. Real, sustained transformation begins with challenging the status quo. To unleash your creativity and your uniqueness, you need to allow yourself to be different and embrace diversity of thought and behavior. Having true character and integrity means that we'd rather be disliked for doing right than being liked for doing wrong. We need to stop conforming to societal standards, which box us in, significantly shrinking our world. We must instead cultivate the idea of thinking and acting differently. We can't ask of others what we ourselves are not willing to give. Leading by example is the only meaningful, effective form of leadership. We must set and operate by our own rules, embracing what makes us different and unique in every facet of our lives. Be a critical thinker; say "no" to blending in; dare to be different. Success smiles upon contrarians, not conformists.

FAIL SMART AND FAST
to win big

3. FAIL SMART AND FAST TO WIN BIG

Are you drained from being stuck, making mistake after mistake, and feeling like you are never moving forward?

All mistakes are not equal. Fail slow and without thinking, and prepare to lose big. Fail smart and fast to win big. There are both dumb and smart failures. There is failing fast and quickly recovering, and there is failing slow, moving backwards and losing faith in oneself. Smart failure means that every mistake works to your advantage and, over time, brings you closer to succeeding. It doesn't hold you back, it boosts your success rate as you reset and apply what you learned. We need to view failure and setbacks as opportunities to strengthen ourselves. By drawing insights from our mistakes, we propel ourselves forward and, over time, become more resilient and better prepared. Stop running away from the fire, and start taking calculated risks. Be open to uncertainty. Be smart and speedy in how you recover from your mistakes.

STOP DREAMING,
start doing

4. STOP DREAMING, START DOING

Are you worn out from watching life pass you by? Or, are you keeping yourself busy but never feeling a sense of real accomplishment?

In life, we must accomplish more if we want to become more. It's that simple. Having an action-oriented attitude ensures we do not get stuck in our own heads, wishing for outcomes that will only materialize if we act. Make things happen now by acting. Create more, consume less. Turn thoughts into action and action into outcomes. Don't overanalyze or overthink. Do not let fear, uncertainty, or change paralyze you. Embrace a life of doing. Fill your days with purposeful activities that move you closer to your goal. Aim high and expect more. Work hard, dream big and be relentless. We are limitless when we are fearless. Do more to get more. Do more to be more.

TREAT TIME
as your most powerful asset

5. TREAT TIME AS YOUR MOST POWERFUL ASSET

Are you weary of wasting time on activities that don't propel you forward? Or going through the day with the feeling that your time wasn't used very wisely?

Time is like hair follicles: you have far less than you think, and you lose more every day. You can't be successful by working part-time or for even a four-day week. This is nonsense. Don't get fooled by time management books that suggest time is your ally, it's not. It's also in short supply, and believe me when I say that it's shrinking faster than common sense. Managing time wisely requires discipline and an early start, which gives you the competitive edge you are likely to need. If you can't make effective use of your time, you won't accomplish ambitious goals you set for yourself. We must use time wisely. It takes practice and dedication to make time work for you. Avoid distractions, always. Learn to say "no" often and apply laser focus to what matters. Time is a fast, depreciating currency to be mastered, not simply managed. No great achievement was ever realized without mastering time. It's a powerful asset. Make the best of it.

SAY "ONCE MORE,"
when others say, "no more"

6. SAY "ONCE MORE" WHEN OTHERS SAY "NO MORE"

Are you tired of seeing others reap the benefits while you sit on the sidelines feeling sorry for yourself—or not knowing when to give it another try before letting go?

When obstacles get in the way or life pushes back and we run out of juice and options, we must stay on task. I promise you this: if it was easy, everyone would do it. It doesn't matter if you are hurt, if you are tired, or if you don't feel like it. You must be self-disciplined. You must be driven. You must be tenacious, determined, committed, and be willing to overcome whatever obstacles are thrown at you. It's often about the last man/woman standing. We must show remarkable resilience. We must keep fighting and never give up. You can't realize great deeds by acting reasonably. Most things in life must be earned. The real challenge of growth and courage is when things don't work out as planned. You may have to start your journey where others stop theirs if you want to go further. The Success Freak in you will be the one answering to the inside voice that says "no more" with a smile.

ALLOW YOUR PASSION
to set you on fire

7. ALLOW YOUR PASSION TO SET YOU ON FIRE.

Are you following your heart and standing up for what you believe in? Are you living your life with a burning passion, feeling like you are making a difference?

Our time on earth is limited, so what kind of legacy will you leave? Don't settle for less than what you absolutely love to do. When our vocation and career align, the impossible becomes possible, and nothing seems hard to accomplish. We think long term and weather any storm, staring firmly at the horizon. If you are not clear about what your passion is, then you are not living, you're merely surviving. There is a light in all of us that never goes out.

Don't confuse passion with career or hobbies. Only once you align what you love with your professional activities will you be on the path to living a remarkable life. There is no compromise possible. Passion is a life worth living, period. It is also a life worth sharing. Let's remember that it's not the possessions we accumulate that make us rich; it's how we positively impact other people's lives.

PROPEL YOURSELF AND KICK ASS - DAY AFTER DAY

Let's be realistic. The journey you started is not just a seven-day adventure that's coming to an end. To the contrary, it's just

194

beginning, but now you are well equipped to see it through. The concept of success is deeply anchored into the notion of "self-awareness" and "creation." If we want to create something of significance that will survive us, we need to know ourselves, and then push past our self-defined limits. Over the years, I've learned that success is a mindset to develop more than it is a skill to acquire. The end of this book is the beginning of a new life chapter that only you can write—by living it mindfully. You are now ready to check your future and make profound changes.

We change the world by being part of it. We change others by loving them. We change ourselves by challenging the status quo. We change our destiny by taking ownership. We change our life by knowing what we want and going after it relentlessly.

With the seven skills you have now acquired, you can propel yourself forward like a rocket eagerly pointing at the sky. We look up, aiming high and leaving footprints in our paths that will be remembered for what we created and more importantly, why we created. It's now time to kick ass in your life and grab what is yours: **an incredibly successful, purposeful life.**

ACTION PLANS

ACTION PLAN

Now that you have completed the exercise section and have reflected on ways you can build this new skill, it's time to act. Here are seven specific actions you must take to immediately apply what you've learned in this chapter:

CHALLENGE ONE:
CREATE YOUR OWN PERSONAL MEASUREMENT OF SUCCESS

☐ Declare what success is to you. Think beyond fame, fortune and other cultural clichés. Write your definition of success down; hang it on your wall; set goals that inspire you. Set yourself free.

☐ Stay true to yourself, no matter what. Resist outside pressures to box you in or to measure yourself by others' expectations.

☐ Prioritize wisely and avoid distractions. Place the big rocks and pebbles in your jar first and make time for what matters most.

☐ Surround yourself with like-minded individuals who are successful on their own terms and encourage others to find their own path.

☐ Trust your instincts and, when in doubt, follow your inner voice.

☐ Don't hold back. Pursue what matters most to you and set realistic milestones for what you aim to achieve.

☐ Tell others how you define your own success, not to challenge or influence them, but to seek their undivided support.

DAY TWO, SKILL TWO
ACTION PLAN

Now that you have completed the exercise section and have reflected on ways you can build this new skill, it's time to act. Here are seven specific actions you must take to immediately apply what you've learned in this chapter:

CHALLENGE TWO:
THINK AND ACT DIFFERENTLY, LIVE BY YOUR OWN RULES

☐ Identify key societal/cultural rules that currently hold you back or make you conform to ideas that are not yours. Learn to suppress them.

☐ Openly challenge the status quo in important aspects of your life. Reexamine what led you to it and consider alternatives.

☐ Allow yourself room to think/act differently. Be rebellious. Reject the most dangerous idea in the world: It has always been done this way.

☐ Pick the road less traveled as needed. Conduct self-awareness and stay true to your internal compass, even if you must travel alone.

☐ Articulate what principles/values must now guide your life and key decisions. Make a list and review before making big decisions.

☐ Understand which rules in your life are negotiable and which are not. Get amazingly good at saying "no" at least once per day. Stay firm under pressure.

☐ Weren't you listening earlier? Ignore rules 1 through 6 and come up with your own. Start thinking different now.

ACTION PLAN

Now that you have completed the exercise section and have reflected on ways you can build this new skill, it's time to act. Here are seven specific actions you must take to immediately apply what you've learned in this chapter:

CHALLENGE THREE:
LEARN TO FAIL SMART AND STRENGTHEN YOUR CHARACTER

☐ Fail forward. Consider every failed attempt moving forward as an opportunity for personal growth and improvement.

☐ Practice makes perfect. Tell yourself "I Will What I Want" and don't give up too early. Keep trying until you make it or learn from it.

☐ Do not waste time pointing fingers at others. Own it. Take full responsibility for your mistakes.

☐ Tell yourself, "Been there, done that." Apply what you've learned immediately. Never repeat the same mistakes twice.

☐ Don't be short-sighted or reckless. Evaluate all your options before making a move. Make sure the end justifies the means.

☐ Look for new learning opportunities. Make risk-taking an integral part of how you manage your life in the future. Push yourself.

☐ Embrace vulnerability and practice humility. Share the findings of your mistakes with people close to you, and learn from theirs, too.

DAY FOUR, SKILL FOUR
ACTION PLAN

Now that you have completed the exercise section and have reflected on ways you can build this new skill, it's time to act.
Here are seven specific actions you must take to immediately apply what you've learned in this chapter:

CHALLENGE FOUR:
BE OBSESSIVELY OUTCOME-ORIENTED

- [ ] Minimize daily distractions by reducing screen time, for example, and avoid wasteful activities (let's be honest: you know what they are)! Free up time to do things that matter.

- [ ] Set clear priorities and measurable goals so you can laser-focus on the most important tasks and activities to propel you forward.

- [ ] Make productive use of your life by working diligently through your to-do list. Infuse your life with action.

- [ ] Do not postpone important tasks that can be done today. Live with a constant sense of urgency. Say no again and again to demands that don't move you forward.

- [ ] Don't overthink to the point of inaction but act with enough knowledge so you are most effective at what you do.

- [ ] When it's time to act, trust your instincts. Favor actionable ideas and tangible results over perfection.

- [ ] Remind yourself that success is never a popularity contest: it's better to be disliked for what we do than loved for what we don't do.

ACTION PLAN

Now that you have completed the exercise section and have
reflected on ways you can build this new skill, it's time to act.
Here are seven specific actions you must take to immediately apply
what you've learned in this chapter:

CHALLENGE FIVE:
ACCOMPLISH MORE BY MASTERING
THE EFFECTIVE USE OF TIME

☐ Remember, success is not a nine-to-five commitment. Start your
day early or finish it late. Make the best use of the limited time
you have.

☐ Focus on being productive with your time. Use productivity tools
and apps to assist. Work smart, not just hard, for better results.

☐ Start removing time-wasters or energy-killers—tasks, people,
thoughts, activities—from your life that are counterproductive,
drain you or steer you away from your end goal.

☐ Visualize your calendar to keep a balanced schedule. Organize
your tasks into short, timed intervals spaced out by short breaks
so you stay energized and on task.

☐ Think about long-term objectives while handling short-term
tasks. Embrace delayed gratification, but only for worthy
purposes.

☐ Follow the 6D rule daily. Adjust your energy level to your
priorities.

☐ Become a professional time master. Turn time into a powerful
asset, not a commodity. Remind those around you to respect
your time.

DAY SIX, SKILL SIX

ACTION PLAN

Now that you have completed the exercise section and have reflected on ways you can build this new skill, it's time to act. Here are seven specific actions you must take to immediately apply what you've learned in this chapter:

CHALLENGE SIX:
DEMONSTRATE UNMATCHED DEDICATION AND RESILIENCE

☐ When things get tough, stay the course. Remember that perfect isn't pretty for anyone and that it takes extraordinary will to accomplish extraordinary things.

☐ Acknowledge that, in the pursuit of goals, pain is inevitable. However, suffering—which is different than pain—is optional. The path to success is not a gentle one.

☐ When you are ready to quit, don't. Listen to your heart instead, not to your muscles, reactions, or self esteem. Keep your eyes on the prize.

☐ Turn every negative thought into a positive one. Remind yourself that nothing of purpose is ever easy. The harder the journey, the more rewarding it will be.

☐ Listen to your inner voice when the path is unclear. Stay away from dream killers or anyone that feels your goals are impossible; show them otherwise.

☐ Like a palm tree, rely on the roots and beliefs you built over the years; remain flexible, but determined, in the face of adversity.

☐ Don't start the day hoping to accomplish something. Just make it happen. Stop using the words "trying" or "wishing" altogether.

DAY SEVEN, SKILL SEVEN
ACTION PLAN

Now that you have completed the exercise section and have reflected on ways you can build this new skill, it's time to act. Here are seven specific actions you must take to immediately apply what you've learned in this chapter:

CHALLENGE SEVEN:
PURSUE A LIFE OF BURNING PASSION AND PURPOSE

☐ Learn what you love to do most; follow your heart; don't give up until you find it.

☐ Declare your vocation and true purpose in life with a passion statement. Use the HOW, WHAT, WHY formula to do so.

☐ Never consider "work" a dirty word again. Instead, explore ways to align your vocation with a career so you can support yourself financially.

☐ Spend most of your time, energy, and efforts on what you love. Stop doing what doesn't nourish your heart and soul. Be selective.

☐ Do not walk, run, or fly blind. Use your passion to influence important life decisions and shed light on your path to success.

☐ Feel right by doing right. Stop pretending or making excuses and choose a life of purpose. Expect happiness as an outcome, not a goal.

☐ Network with individuals who share a common passion. Communicate, collaborate, and share, making your passion contagious.

RESOURCES

Introduction

Ryan, Camille L. & Bauman, Kurt. "2015 Population Characteristics, Current Population Reports," Educational Attainment in the United States (March 2016 Census). P20-578 https://www.census.gov/content/dam/Census/library/publications/2016/demo/p20-578.pdf.

World Happiness Report (2017). http://worldhappiness.report/wp-content/uploads/sites/2/2017/03/HR17-Ch7.pdf.

"World Happiness Report." n.d. Wikipedia. Accessed May 14, 2017. https://en.wikipedia.org/wiki/World_Happiness_Report.

Chapter 1

"Success." n.d. Merriam-Webster. Accessed March 26, 2017. https://www.merriam-webster.com/dictionary/success.

B., Joshua. 2014. "10 Of the World's Most Tragic Suicides." The Richest. June 8, 2014. https://www.therichest.com/rich-list/most-shocking/10-of-the-worlds-most-tragic-suicides/.

"J.K. Rowling." n.d. Wikipedia. Accessed October 23, 2016. https://en.wikipedia.org/wiki/J._K._Rowling.

Narayan, Lux. What I learned from 2,000 obituaries - TED Talk, Posted March 2017 http://www.ted.com/talks/lux_narayan_what_i_learned_from_2_000_obituaries?language=en

Fox, Michelle. 2013. "People Who Quit Their Jobs and Made Millions." CNBC. February 27, 2013. https://www.cnbc.com/2012/01/23/People-Who-Quit-Their-Jobs-and-Made-Millions.html?slide=1.

Generation Wealth (aka Wealth: The Influence of Affluence), Documentary, written and directed by Lauren Greenfield, Amazon Studios, Elevation Pictures, July 20, 2018.

Baer, Drake. 2014. "How 9 Incredibly Successful People Define Success." Business Insider. June 2, 2014. https://www.businessinsider.com/how-9-incredibly-successful-people-define-success-2014-5.

Brickman, Philip and Coates, Dan, Northwestern University, Ronnie Jaroff-Bulman, University of Massachusetts

Brickman, Philip, Dan Coates, and Ronnie Jaroff-Bulman. 1978. "Lottery Winners and Accident Victims: Is Happiness Relative?" *Journal of Personality and Social Psychology*, 917-927, 36 (8).

Chopra, Deepak. 1994. *The Seven Spiritual Laws of Success*. Amber-Allen Publishing.

"Our Promise." n.d. Method. Accessed March 26, 2017. http://methodhome.com/about-us/our-promise/.

"Harry Potter (Film Series)." n.d. Wikipedia. Accessed June 16, 2017. https://en.wikipedia.org/wiki/Harry_Potter_(film_series).

Russell, Kaitlyn. 2017. "25 Steve Jobs Quotes That Will Change the Way You Work—in the Best Way Possible." The Muse. June 16, 2017. https://www.themuse.com/advice/25-steve-jobs-quotes-that-will-change-the-way-you-workin-the-best-way-possible.

"Top Influencers." 2019. Forbes. 2019. https://www.forbes.com/top-influencers/#2eaa7df572dd.

O'Connor, Clare. 2017. "Forbes Top Influencers: Instagram 'It' Girl Chiara Ferragni On Building A Fashion Empire." Forbes. September 26, 2017. https://www.forbes.com/sites/clareoconnor/2017/09/26/forbes-top-influencers-instagram-it-girl-chiara-ferragni-on-building-a-fashion-empire/#398d81073001.

The Telegraph. 2017. "The Highest-Paid Instagram Influencers, Including One Star Who Gets £14,000 per Post," July 19, 2017. https://www.telegraph.co.uk/business/0/highest-paid-instagram-influencers-including-one-star-gets-14000/picture-instagram-user-chiara-ferragni/.

"Chiara Ferragni." n.d. Wikipedia. Accessed February 4, 2019. https://en.wikipedia.org/wiki/Chiara_Ferragni.

Kahneman, Daniel, and Angus Deaton. 2010. "High Income Improves Evaluation of Life but Not Emotional Well-Being." PNAS. September 21, 2010. https://www.pnas.org/content/107/38/16489.full?sid=a5db21e9-4c43-48eb-97b1-df31fe3f3074.

"Nike: Dream Crazy." 2018. Wieden Kennedy. September 2018. https://www.wk.com/work/nike-dream-crazy/.

AAPPC, Poison Center Data Snapshot 2015, Annual Report of the American Association of Poison Control Centers' National Poison Data System (NPDS): 32nd Annual Report. Clin Toxicol (Phila). 2016, https://aapcc.s3.amazonaws.com/pdfs/annual_reports/2015_Annual_Report_Snapshot_FINAL_1-17-17.pdf

Mejia, Zameena. 2018. "Warren Buffett Says This Is His Measure of Success—and It Helped Bill Gates in 2018." CNBC. December 31, 2018. https://www.cnbc.com/2018/12/31/how-warren-buffetts-measure-of-success-shaped-2018-for-bill-gates.html?&qsearchterm=Warren Buffett says this is his measure of success—and it helped Bill Gates in 2018.

Chapter 2

Chuck Yeager. http://www.chuckyeager.com/.

"Think Different." n.d. Wikipedia. Accessed January 14, 2017. https://en.wikipedia.org/wiki/Think_different.

"Character." n.d. Wikipedia. Accessed March 26, 2017. https://en.wiktionary.org/wiki/character.

"Rosa Parks." n.d. Wikipedia. Accessed February 17, 2019. https://en.wikipedia.org/wiki/Rosa_Parks.

"Think Different." n.d. The Crazy Ones. Accessed January 14, 2017. http://www.thecrazyones. it/spot-en.html.

Brown, Derren. Netflix Original *The Push*. Reality TV, 2018

Van Praag, Joshua , Martinez, Raoul. Lottery of Birth, History/documentary, IMDB, Initial release: September 27, 2012. 1h 17m, http://www.imdb.com/title/tt2294551/

Snyder Bulik, Beth. 2010. "Marketer of the Decade: Apple." *Ad Age*, October 18, 2010.

"Richard Branson." n.d. Wikipedia. Accessed March 26, 2017. https://en.wikipedia.org/wiki/ Richard_Branson.

Young, Lauren. 2016. "Why This Groundbreaking British Doctor Was Almost Erased From the History Books." *Atlas Obscura*, December 22, 2016. https://www.atlasobscura.com/ articles/dr-james-barry-gender.

"Coco Chanel." n.d. Wikipedia. Accessed October 22, 2017. https://en.wikipedia.org/wiki/ Coco_Chanel.

Chapter 3

Shedd, John A. 1928. *Salt from My Attic*. Mosher Press.

http://study.com/academy/lesson/fundamental-attribution-error-definition-lesson-quiz.html From Study.com, accessed Tues March 7, 2017

https://hbr.org/archive-toc/BR1104

Grant, Adam. The surprising habits of original thinkers, TED2016 · 15:25 · Filmed Feb 2016, https://www.ted.com/talks/adam_grant_the_surprising_habits_of_original_thinkers/ transcript?language=en

"Aaron Kozbelt." n.d. Brooklyn College. Accessed April 27, 2019. http://www.brooklyn.cuny. edu/web/academics/faculty/faculty_profile.jsp?faculty=437.

Henion, Andy, Moser, Jason. Learning From Our Mistakes is Hardwired. Michigan State University. Published: Oct. 3, 2011. http://msutoday.msu.edu/news/2011/learning-from-our-mistakes-is-hardwired/

"List of Edison Patents." n.d. Wikipedia. Accessed June 16, 2017. https://en.wikipedia.org/ wiki/List_of_Edison_patents.

Misty Copeland. Accessed June 16, 2017. http://mistycopeland.com/.

McCarthy, Michael. 2014. "Ad of the Day: Ballerina Misty Copeland Stars in Jaw-Dropping Spot for Under Armour." *Adweek*, August 1, 2014. http://www.adweek. com/brand-marketing/ad-day-ballerina-misty-copeland-stars-jaw-dropping-spot-under-armour-159235/

Kristiano, Ang. 2017. "Proof That Americans Are Really Obsessed with How They Smell." *New York Post*, June 21, 2017.

Breyer, Melissa. 2016. "6 Glorious Benefits of Sweating." TreeHugger. July 20, 2016. https:// www.treehugger.com/health/6-glorious-benefits-of-sweating.html.

Williams-Grut, Oscar. 2017. "Amazon Innovation Chief: 'We Are Failing and Will Continue to Fail'." *Business Insider*, September 15, 2017. https://www.businessinsider.com/ amazon-failure-innovation-2017-9.

Under Armour campaign "I will what I want," Droga5, 2018, https://droga5.com/work/under-armour/. Last accessed April 27, 2019

Steinberg, Neil. 2017. "How to Fall to Your Death and Live to Tell the Tale." Mosaic Science. June 6, 2017. https://mosaicscience.com/story/falling-science-injury-death-falls/.

Exploratorium, The Science of Hockey, https://www.exploratorium.edu/hockey/skating2.html. Last access August 14, 2017

Chapter 4

Estee Launder Companies. "The Estee Story," https://www.elcompanies.com/en/who-we-are/the-lauder-family/the-estee-story, last accessed 6/21/2019

Enderle, Kim, Dan Hirsch, Lisa Micka, Brian Saving, Sheetal Shah, and Tatiana Szerwinski. 2000. "Strategic Analysis of Nike, Inc." DePaul University. March 14, 2000. http://condor.depaul.edu/aalmaney/StrategicAnalysisofNike.htm.

"Nike, Inc." n.d. Wikipedia. Accessed September 10, 2017.

"Just Do It." n.d. Wikipedia. Accessed September 10, 2017. https://en.wikipedia.org/wiki/Just_Do_It.

Tolle, Eckhart. 2010. *The Power of Now: A Guide to Spiritual Enlightenment*. New World Library.

Cliggett, Mark. 2004. "Microsoft Values." Web log. *Microsoft Developer Network* (blog). March 19, 2004. https://blogs.msdn.microsoft.com/markcli/2004/03/19/microsoft-values/.

Allen, David. 2002. *Getting Things Done: The Art of Stress-Free Productivity*. Reprint ed. Penguin Books.

Tracy, Brian. 2007. *Eat That Frog!: 21 Great Ways to Stop Procrastinating and Get More Done in Less Time*. 2nd ed. Berrett-Koehler Publishers.

Montero, Barbara Gail. 2013. "The Myth of 'Just Do It.'" *New York Times*, June 9, 2013.

Wilson, Timothy, and Jonathan Schooler. 1991. "Thinking Too Much: Introspection Can Reduce the Quality of Preferences and Decisions [Attitudes and Social Cognition]." *Journal of Personality and Social Psychology*, 181-92, 60 (2). https://doi.org/10.1037//0022-3514.60.2.181

Gladwell, Malcolm. 2007. *Blink: The Power of Thinking Without Thinking*. 1st ed. Back Bay Books.

Elkins, Kathleen. 2015. "Billionaire John Paul DeJoria Says the Smartest Thing He's Ever Done with His Money Is a Habit He Started at Age 6." *Business Insider*, December 9, 2015. https://www.businessinsider.com/smartest-thing-john-paul-dejoria-did-with-money-2015-12.

"John Paul DeJoria." n.d. Wikipedia. Accessed April 15, 2017. https://en.wikipedia.org/wiki/John_Paul_DeJoria.

"Galileo Galilei." n.d. Wikipedia. Accessed April 15, 2017. https://en.wikipedia.org/wiki/Galileo_Galilei.

"Helen Keller." n.d. Wikipedia. Accessed April 15, 2017. https://en.wikipedia.org/wiki/Helen_Keller.

Shit or get off the pot, Wikipedia, https://en.wikipedia.org/wiki/Shit_or_get_off_the_pot, last accessed June 17, 2017

Culture at Netflix, https://jobs.netflix.com/culture, last accessed August 15, 2017

"Leadership Principles." n.d. Amazon. Accessed August 15, 2017. https://www.amazon.jobs/en/principles.

"The Science Behind Success." 2016. Ellory Wells. August 1, 2016. https://www.ellorywells.com/math-science-success/.

"Analysis Paralysis." n.d. Wikipedia. Accessed August 15, 2017. https://en.wikipedia.org/wiki/Analysis_paralysis.

Roberts, Lon. 2010. "Analysis Paralysis: A Case of Terminological Inexactitude." *Defense Acquisition Magazine*, 2010. Defense Acquisition University. https://web.archive.org/web/20170131231704/http://www.dau.mil/pubscats/ATL Docs/Jan-Feb/robersts_jan-feb10.pdf.

A Great Big Story channel video inspired by Genesis, "How the Inventor of the Rubik's Cube Cracked His Own Code," YouTube, https://www.youtube.com/watch?v=l_-QxnzK4gM

Rubik's. Accessed October 14, 2017. https://www.rubiks.com/about.

"Ernő Rubik." n.d. Wikipedia. Accessed October 14, 2017. https://en.wikipedia.org/wiki/Ernő_Rubik.

Chapter 5

Mischel, Walter. 2014. *The Marshmallow Test: Mastering Self-Control*. Little, Brown and Company.

"It's Five O'Clock Somewhere." n.d. Wikipedia. Accessed April 16, 2017. https://en.wikipedia.org/wiki/It's_Five_O'Clock_Somewhere.

Lazovick, Meg. 2015. "Wake Me up: What Time Do Americans Start Their Day?" Edison Research. March 26, 2015. http://www.edisonresearch.com/wake-me-up-series-2/.

Thoreau, Henry David. Letter to Harrison Blake (Concord, November 16, 1857)

de La Bruyère, Jean. Characters, XII. Of Opinions, Scribner & Welford, 1885 and BARTLEBY.COM, 2011

Citrin, Jim. 2007. "Tapping the Power of Your Morning Routine." Yahoo! Finance. January 30, 2007. http://web.archive.org/web/20101205195210/http://finance.yahoo.com/expert/article/leadership/23188.

Goldschein, Eric, and Gus Lubin. 2012. "23 Successful People Who Wake Up Really Early." *Business Insider*, January 11, 2012. https://www.businessinsider.com/successful-early-risers-2012-1.

Henry, Alan. 2014. "Productivity 101: A Primer to The Pomodoro Technique." Lifehacker. July 2, 2014. http://lifehacker.com/productivity-101-a-primer-to-the-pomodoro-technique-1598992730.

Cirillo, Francesco. 2013. *The Pomodoro Technique*. 3rd ed. FC Garage GmbH.

Ferriss, Timothy. 2016. *Tools of Titans: The Tactics, Routines, and Habits of Billionaires, Icons, and World-Class Performers*. Houghton Mifflin Harcourt.

Nardelli, Alberto. 2015. "The French Take More Holidays and Work Less—but Does It Matter?" *The Guardian*, June 5, 2015. https://www.theguardian.com/news/datablog/2015/jun/05/french-more-holidays-work-less-productivity.

"List of Countries by GDP (PPP) per Hour Worked." n.d. Wikipedia. Accessed August 15, 2017. https://en.wikipedia.org/wiki/List_of_countries_by_GDP_(PPP)_per_hour_worked.

Kondo, Marie. 2014. *The Life-Changing Magic of Tidying Up: The Japanese Art of Decluttering and Organizing*. 1st ed. Ten Speed Press.

Barker, Eric. 2017. "The Science Behind Success And Motivation." *Forbes*, May 19, 2017. https://www.forbes.com/sites/quora/2017/05/19/the-science-behind-success-and-motivation/#511c07ac44a8.

"Working Time." n.d. Wikipedia. Accessed August 15, 2017. https://en.wikipedia.org/wiki/Working_time.

Thrive Global. Jeff Bezos: Why Getting 8 Hours of Sleep Is Good for Amazon Shareholders, Thrive Global, November 30, 2016, https://journal.thriveglobal.com/jeff-bezos-sleep-amazon-19c617c59daa

"Jeff Bezos: Why Getting 8 Hours of Sleep Is Good for Amazon Shareholders." 2016. Thrive Global. November 30, 2016. https://journal.thriveglobal.com/jeff-bezos-sleep-amazon-19c617c59daa.

Gazzaley, Adam, and Larry D. Rosen. 2016. *The Distracted Mind: Ancient Brains in a High-Tech World*. MIT Press.

Getting Things Done. Accessed October 15, 2017. http://gettingthingsdone.com/.

Ericsson, K. Anders, Ralf Th. Krampe, and Clemens Tesch-Römer. 1993. "The Role of Deliberate Practice in the Acquisition of Expert Performance." *Psychological Review*, 363-406, 100 (3).

"Sleep Deprivation." n.d. Wikipedia. Accessed August 17, 2017. https://en.wikipedia.org/wiki/Sleep_deprivation.

Amabile, Teresa, and Steven J. Kramer. 2011. "The Power of Small Wins." *Harvard Business Review*, May 2011. https://hbr.org/2011/05/the-power-of-small-wins.

"About Teresa Amabile." n.d. The Progress Principle. Accessed October 22, 2017. http://progressprinciple.com/bio/teresa-amabile.

Chapter 6

Dvorsky, George. 2016. "Scientists Finally Figured Out Why Tardigrades Are So Indestructible." Gizmodo. September 20, 2016. http://gizmodo.com/genes-hold-the-key-to-the-water-bears-indestructibility-1786814698.

Gillette's Perfect Isn't Pretty Film Pays Tribute to Arduous Journeys Faced by Athletes in Lead up to Rio 2016 Olympic Games, Film - July 13, 2016, http://news.pg.com/press-release/pg-corporate-announcements/gillettes-perfect-isnt-pretty-film-pays-tribute-arduous-jou

The Barkley Marathons: The Race That Eats Its Young (2014) - 1h 29min | Documentary, Adventure, History | 1 October 2016, IMDb, http://www.imdb.com/title/tt2400291/ and https://en.wikipedia.org/wiki/Barkley_Marathons last accessed 4/23/2017

Duckworth, Angela L. (University of Pennsylvania), Peterson, Christopher (University of Michigan), Matthews, Michael D. and Kelly, Dennis R. Grit: Perseverance and Passion for Long-Term Goals, United States Military Academy, West Point, 2007, https://www.sas.upenn.edu/~duckwort/images/Grit%20JPSP.pdf

Nietzsche, Friedrich. 1889. *Twilight of the Idols*.

Economy, Peter. 2017. "These 11 Elon Musk Quotes Will Inspire Your Success and Happiness." *Inc.*, October 24, 2017. https://www.inc.com/peter-economy/11-elon-musk-quotes-that-will-push-you-to-achieve-impossible.html.

Breyer, Melissa. 2016. "How Do Palm Trees Survive Hurricanes?" TreeHugger. October 6, 2016. https://www.treehugger.com/natural-sciences/how-do-palm-trees-survive-hurricanes.html.

"Saffir–Simpson Scale." n.d. Wikipedia. Accessed August 18, 2017. https://en.wikipedia.org/wiki/Saffir–Simpson_scale.

Chapter 7

Vallerand, Robert J. 2012. "The Role of Passion in Sustainable Psychological Well-Being." *Psychology of Well-Being: Theory, Research and Practice*, March. https://doi.org/https://doi.org/10.1186/2211-1522-2-1.

"List of Nobel Laureates." n.d. Wikipedia. Accessed May 6, 2017. https://en.wikipedia.org/wiki/List_of_Nobel_laureates.

"List of Lifetime Achievement Awards." n.d. Wikipedia. Accessed May 6, 2017. https://en.wikipedia.org/wiki/List_of_lifetime_achievement_awards.

Hegel, Georg Wilhem Friedrich. 1894. *Lectures on the Philosophy of History*. George Bell & Sons.

"Ikigai." n.d. Wikipedia. Accessed May 14, 2017. https://en.wikipedia.org/wiki/Ikigai.

About TED, TED.com, last accessed May 14, 2017. https://www.ted.com/about/our-organization

Kalb, Claudia. 2017. "What Makes a Genius?" *National Geographic*, May 2017. https://www.nationalgeographic.com/magazine/2017/05/genius-genetics-intelligence-neuroscience-creativity-einstein/.

Sonnad, Nikhil. 2017. "Wikipedia's Great Experiment: Finding a Definition of 'Happiness' We Can All Agree On." Quartz. April 18, 2017. https://qz.com/912028/why-happiness-is-difficult-to-define-wikipedias-answer-is-the-result-of-6000-edits-by-over-3000-users/.

Smith, Emily Esfahani. 2017. *The Power of Meaning: Crafting a Life That Matters*. Crown.

Frankl, Viktor E. 2006. *Man's Search for Meaning*. 1st ed. Beacon Pres.

"Viktor Frankl." n.d. Wikipedia. Accessed April 21, 2019. https://en.wikipedia.org/wiki/Viktor_Frankl.

"Denzel Washington." n.d. Wikipedia. Accessed August 19, 2017. https://en.wikipedia.org/wiki/Denzel_Washington.

Transcript of Denzel Washington's commencement ceremony speech to college graduates at the Dillard University, May 9, 2015 https://speakola.com/grad/denzel-washington-everything-i-have-is-by-the-grace-of-god-full-2015

Transcript of Jim Carrey's Commencement Address at the 2014 MUM Graduation, Maharishi University of Management, video published on May 30, 2014, https://www.youtube.com/watch?v=V80-gPkpH6M

Macek III, J. C. 2012. "Bless This Mess: Sweeping the Kitchen With Julia Child." *PopMatters*, August 12, 2012. https://www.popmatters.com/161490-bless-this-mess-sweeping-the-kitchen-with-julia-child-2495828420.html.

"A Look Back ... Julia Child: Life Before French Cuisine." 2007. Central Intelligence Agency. September 13, 2007. https://www.cia.gov/news-information/featured-story-archive/2007-featured-story-archive/julia-child.html.

People. 1998. "Andrea Bocelli: Singer," May 11, 1998. https://people.com/archive/andrea-bocelli-singer-vol-49-no-18/.

Rogers, Paul. 2013. "Andrea Bocelli at the MGM Grand." *Los Angeles Time*, September 5, 2013. https://www.latimes.com/brandpublishing/travelplus/lasvegasguide/features/la-ss-andrea-bocelli-at-the-mgm-grand-20130904-dto-story.html.

Day, Carol. 1997. "Blind Ambition." *People*, November 10, 1997. https://people.com/archive/blind-ambition-vol-48-no-19/.

"Andrea Bocelli." n.d. Wikipedia. Accessed April 21, 2019. https://en.wikipedia.org/wiki/Andrea_Bocelli.

Macek III, J. C. 2012. "Bless This Mess: Sweeping the Kitchen With Julia Child." *PopMatters*, August 12, 2012. https://www.popmatters.com/161490-bless-this-mess-sweeping-the-kitchen-with-julia-child-2495828420.html.

Patrick, Jeanette. The Recipe for Adventure: Chef Julia Child's World War II Service," National Women's History Museum, 2017

"Julia Child." n.d. Wikipedia. Accessed April 21, 2019. https://en.wikipedia.org/wiki/Julia_Child.

Conclusion

How Ants Use Vision When Homing Backward, By Sebastian Schwarz, Michael Mangan, Jochen Zeil, Barbara Webb, Antoine Wystrach, Cell, Current Biology, Published Online: January 19, 2017, http://www.cell.com/current-biology/abstract/S0960-9822(16)31466-X

Botkin-Kowacki, Eva. 2017. "Able Navigators: How Desert Ants Know Which Way to Go When Walking Backward." *The Christian Science Monitor*, January 20, 2017. https://www.csmonitor.com/Science/2017/0120/Able-navigators-How-desert-ants-know-which-way-to-go-when-walking-backward.

"Ant." n.d. Wikipedia. Accessed July 19, 2017. https://en.wikipedia.org/wiki/Ant.

Epictetus, The Discourses of Epictetus, Book II, ch. 17. Elizabeth Carter translation, 1759

Kalb, Claudia. 2017. "What Makes a Genius?" *National Geographic*, May 2017. https://www.nationalgeographic.com/magazine/2017/05/genius-genetics-intelligence-neuroscience-creativity-einstein/.

ONLINE RESOURCES

To download templates and access additional resources to bring
your new skills to life:

http://www.successfreakbook.com/tools
Password: mysuccess

ABOUT THE AUTHOR

A seasoned and award-winning business executive, Bruno Gralpois has over twenty-five years of Fortune 100, high-tech, and entrepreneurial experience. He's been featured in media outlets, radio, and television shows for his innovative thinking and thought leadership. Gralpois has worked with the most prestigious brands in the world including Microsoft, Visa, Toyota, Verizon, P&G, Dell, and many others steering partnerships in excess of $1 billion.

A French native, Gralpois co-founded Seattle-based service and technology firm, Agency Mania Solutions, which works with the world's largest brands. Gralpois was previously the Head of Global Marketing Operations at Visa Inc. and Director of Global Agency Strategy at Microsoft, where he spent a decade. Among other noteworthy accomplishments, he received the prestigious Microsoft Marketing Excellence Award from then Microsoft CEO Steve Ballmer. A serial entrepreneur and innovator, he also held leadership positions in successful pre- and post-IPO high-tech companies. Gralpois holds an MBA in Marketing and International Business, and is a former French Foreign Trade Advisor. He's a frequent speaker at industry events. He's the author of *Magnifique: Inside & Out* and *Agency Mania* (1st and 2nd edition)—considered a reference book in the business community. As a faculty member of the Association of National Advertisers, he has trained countless Fortune 100 companies. For more information about the author of *Success Freak*, visit www.brunogralpois.com. Follow him on Twitter (@gralpois), Instagram (brunogralpois), LinkedIn (http://www.linkedin.com/in/gralpois/) or Facebook (www.facebook.com/successfreakbook/).

Michael Curtis Photography
michaelcurtisphotography.com